THE DOMAIN OF IDEOLOGIES
A Study of the Origin, Development and Structure of Ideologies

Harold Walsby

Cover Design by Kevin I. Slaughter

First Impression: August 1946
Riverside Press Ltd., Thwickenham, Middlesex

Second Impression: January 2020
George Walford International Essay Prize
Trevor Blake, P. O. Box 2321, Portland OR 97208 United States

Walsby, Harold
[English]
Domain of Ideologies, The
ISBN 978-1-944651-15-2
1. Philosophy
2. Political Science
Harold Walsby (1911 - 1973); George Walford (1919 - 1994); Trevor
Blake (b. 1966)

An Outline Sketch of Systematic Ideology by George Walford. Previously published in London at The Bookshop, 1977.

The George Walford International Essay Prize is an annual essay
competition in memory of George Walford. The subject of the essay is
systematic ideology and the prize is £3,500 for the winner to spend
at the college and on the course of the winner's choice. Everything
necessary to apply for, research and win this Prize can be found at ...

gwiep.net

127 House: At every turn in its thought society will find us waiting.

Harold Walsby (circa 1950)

4

Contents

Dedication

TO F. S. JOHNSON

8

Foreword

FOR well over ten years now I have been deeply interested in a field of study which, generally speaking, has so far received comparatively little attention and practically no systematic investigation from men of the scientific frame of mind: the domain of ideologies. This realm – a realm of ascertainable fact and natural phenomena like any other part of existence – is for science, at any rate, a relatively new and unexplored territory. It is the realm of the various, more or less familiar and everyday "mental attitudes-to-life" and "world-outlooks" – including the almost unknown, uncharted region of their psychobiological origins, their structures, relations, mode of development and so on.

The reasons for this scant interest in the subject on the part of science, whatever they are, can hardly be centred in an intrinsic unworthiness of the subject-matter to be accorded serious scientific consideration and treatment. The numerous appeals, hints, pointings, tentative gropings and suggestions – with regard to the vital necessity of such a branch of scientific study – which appear, tucked away in the pages of the last decade's many books on social and political questions, testify to that. Moreover, since the sudden and disquieting arrival of atomic energy as a source of power, it has become increasingly evident that, to quite a number of people, at least, who think about the future of our present civilisation, the need for the development of a science of human social consciousness is long overdue – even dangerously so.

What follows in this book – breaking, as it does, much that is virgin ground – is a humble endeavour, on the one hand, to stimulate a wider objective interest in the subject and a wider appreciation of the social importance of this field of study, and on the other hand, to make some concrete contribution towards the filling-in of what amounts to a grave and broad lacuna in the general body of systematised knowledge.

Hitherto, the study of the intellectual-emotional attitudes, or ideologies of social groups has been left very largely to philosophy, to historians and to literary speculation. Ethnologists and psychologists have here and there touched upon the subject, but only upon particular aspects and problems which arise in connection with their own subject-matter. The objective study of ideologies in general, as a distinct and legitimate field of study – existing, so to speak, in its own right – has still to be widely recognised.

Yet the beginnings of this recognition take us back over half a century to the time of Marx, Engels and Morgan. We may remind the reader of the important discovery by these three (jointly, to a great extent, by Marx and Engels, and independently by Lewis H. Morgan in America): the discovery of the enormous conditioning influence exercised, throughout history and prehistory, by the changing economic environment of men upon the *contents* of their thought, and through the medium of these latter, upon their social activities, products and institutions. This discovery was so far-reaching and fruitful in its many applications and was applied so thoroughly and relentlessly – and even, as we shall see, so exclusively – by Marx, Engels and their followers, that it quite overshadowed and thrust into the background the possibility of an independent study of the typical, inherent *forms* or *modes* of men's thought and the influence of *these* upon society.

The result tended to be one-sided: an over-emphasis and over-estimation of the economic factor – particularly for later students of Marxism and many others who later came under its slowly-spreading intellectual influence. The recognised psychology of the period, we must remember, was hardly more than descriptive and very superficial. However, that this over-emphasis of economic conditioning as final and ultimate was no mere historical accident or oversight, we propose to show in the course of the following pages.

Two years before he died, Engels admitted "the mistake" in a letter to Marx's biographer, Mehring:

> Otherwise there is only one other point lacking, which, however, Marx and I always failed to stress enough in our writings and in, regard to which we are all equally guilty. We all, that is to say, laid and were bound to lay the main emphasis at first on the derivation of political, juridical and other ideological notions, and of the actions arising through the medium of these notions from basic economic facts. But in so doing we neglected the formal side-the way in which these notions came about – for the sake of the content... Ideology is a process accomplished by the so-called thinker consciously, indeed, but with a false consciousness. The real motives impelling him remain unknown to him, otherwise it would not be an ideological process at all. Hence he imagines false or apparent motives... This side of the matter, which I can only indicate here, we have all, I think, neglected more than it deserves. It is the old story: form is always neglected at first for content. As I say, I have done that too, and the mistake has always only struck me later. (p. 510, *Marx-Engels Selected Correspondence*.)

Despite the comparatively early date (1893) of this realisation by Engels of the possibility of an objective study of ideological *forms* or *modes*, as distinguished from the study of their *content* or *subject-matter*, very little or nothing has been forthcoming since that time to show that any concentrated attack has been made on the problem. Perhaps this is not in itself wholly surprising, since the matter had largely to wait on the development of individual psychology and the discoveries which have been made in that field since Engels' day.

Engels' statement that "Ideology is a process accomplished... with a false consciousness... The real motives impelling him remain unknown to him, otherwise it would not be an ideological process at all" shows astonishing insight in view of the later psychological discoveries by Freud concerning unconscious motivation, and is entirely in harmony with the contents of the present volume. That this insight into the fundamental nature of the ideological process was in large measure due to Hegel's great influence upon him we can scarcely doubt. Thus in his *Ludwig Feuerbach* Engels praises Hegel's fine work *The Phenomenology of Mind* as "a parallel of the embryology and palaeontology of the mind, a development of the individual consciousness through its different stages, couched in the form of an abbreviated recapitulation of the stages through which the consciousness of man has passed in the course of history... "

This latter conception of a continuous development of the ideological process through a series of successive stages, levels or layers, occupies a prominent place in the ensuing pages, as does also the further Hegelian (and psychoanalytic) conception of the coexistence of mental stages or levels of development. We are, in fact, confronted with a structure or system of coexistent ideological layers. When we come to examine their history we shall find that the ideological layers have grown, or evolved, one out of the other. Each layer – which can be regarded as a level of mental organisation – contains within itself a more or less distinctive and basic set of assumptions, or presuppositions, to which those who occupy the layer are largely unconsciously attached by the emotional tie of identification. Again, these differing but related sets of assumptions, which underlie and colour the various political and philosophical interpretations of events, indicate stages in the development of a continuous repressive process beginning with the birth of each individual.

It will thus readily be seen that the concepts of ideological development and layer-structure can be traced back as far as Hegel. The concepts of repression, identification, introjection, projection etc., which enable us to explain much of the layer-structure and the actual ideological process itself – i.e. "the way in which these notions came about" (see Engels above) – such concepts, we have, of course, drawn from psychoanalysis.

Apart from these vigorous and fruitful sources, there is another, equally dynamic and fruitful, namely, Pavlovian reflexology – or Russian behaviourism, as it is sometimes called – upon which we have freely drawn for factual material in connection with the problem of assumption and the derivation of the assumptive process.

These various influences, then, were the main ones under which the whole subject of ideologies was eventually approached, and under which the following chapters came to be written. These influences show themselves more clearly, perhaps, in Part II – which deals with ideological structure and development – than they do in Part I which treats of the characteristics and relations of mass groups and intellectual groups.

In conclusion I must apologise to the reader for the over-large amount of quotations which have been embodied in the text of Part I. I can only plead that, owing to the special nature of the subject, these quotations constitute the direct ideological evidence, and are more or less unavoidable if the main contentions are to be properly established.

H. W.
Hampstead,
London,
1946.

Part I

Mass Groups and Intellectual Groups

1.1 The Paradox

The more the ordinary mind takes the opposition between true and false to be fixed, the more it is accustomed to expect either agreement or contradiction with a given philosophical system, and only to see reason for the one or the other in any explanatory statement concerning such a system. It does not conceive the diversity of philosophical systems as the progressive evolution of truth; rather, it sees only contradiction in that variety. The bud disappears when the blossom breaks through, and we might say that the former is refuted by the latter; in the same way, when the fruit comes, the blossom may be explained to be a false form of the plant's existence, for the fruit appears as its true nature in place of the blossom. These stages are not merely differentiated; they supplant one another as being incompatible with one another. But the ceaseless activity of their own inherent nature makes them at the same time moments of an organic unity, where they not merely do not contradict one another, but where one is as necessary as the other; and this equal necessity of all moments constitutes alone and thereby the life of the whole. But contradiction as between philosophical systems is not wont to be conceived in this way; on the other hand, the mind, perceiving the contradiction does not commonly know how to relieve it or keep it free from its onesidedness, and to recognise in what seems conflicting and inherently antagonistic the presence of mutually necessary moment.

– Hegel, *The Phenomenology of Mind.*

I N taking general stock of the world as it exists today no intelligent being could remain unimpressed by the unique and increasingly important position occupied by science. Again, in making the most, casual comparisons with the past, nothing is more evident than that the direct influence of scientific activity upon our everyday life is growing apace; that, historically speaking, more and more of the world around us is rapidly coming under its control; that great changes in our way of living are being effected by science in ever shorter periods of time. From all sides we are continually being reminded that we live in a scientific age.

Furthermore, we are told, this is but a tithe of what is possible and what is to come – and evidently with some truth, for there is not immediately apparent any comprehensive limit (though we may feel there must be one) to the growth of science on the one hand, or to the rapidity of its development and expansion, on the other.

Yet, strangely enough, this great increase in the mastery of our environment is attended by a most extraordinary and outstanding contradiction. For the application by man of his new power largely results in making life less secure and more hazardous for the great mass of the people. With this increasing control over our environment, provided for us in the first place by science, we ourselves become more and more like straws raised by the blast of the ever-quickening tempo of scientific and technological development. "It cannot be denied," said Sir Arthur Eddington, in his *New Pathways in Science*, "that for a society which has to create scarcity to save its members from starvation, to whom abundance spells disaster, and to whom unlimited energy means unlimited power for war and destruction, there is an ominous cloud in the distance though at present it be no bigger than a man's hand."

Moreover, the scientists themselves are not, on the whole, secluded from this unintentional effect of the new forces they have produced; and, in point of fact, as a consequence of it, find their scientific labours in many ways frustrated. The risks and uncertainties arising from the peculiar nature of life in modern society are shared (if not equally, at least to some extent) by the overwhelming majority, especially in wartime. Poverty, unemployment, malnutrition, industrial disease, bodily injury and violent death – to mention some of the worst features – are only too common and too well-known in this vaunted age of science to need any description or emphasis. Those who are not either visited by or exposed to any of these conditions are few indeed.

Are these social evils a necessary consequence of scientific development? Are they, as some suppose, the price we have to pay for too much science?

When we consider the enormous and growing power that science is placing at our disposal; when we think of the innumerable ways, means and methods given us by modern science, whereby we are enabled, with increasing rapidity, to alter and adapt our material environment to our needs, i.e., to produce abundant wealth; when at the same time we realise that the practical use to which these discoveries are put is left mainly to a class of private individuals whose prime aim, in deciding whether to exploit or suppress an invention, is to make as much money for themselves as possible; when, in addition, we realise that the administration of affairs arising out of these conditions is in the hands of men, no doubt well-meaning but with relatively no scientific knowledge or understanding of the real problems they are called upon to solve, and who have been elected to office by largely ignorant, indiscriminating and unscientifically-minded masses – when we reflect upon all this then I think we must conclude that the evil is not too much science but rather too little.

"If, then," wrote the psychologist McDougall, "we have reason to be profoundly dissatisfied with the state of our civilization, we shall do well to consider whether there is not some radical defect in our knowledge, more especially in the systematically organised part of our knowledge we call Science." And again: "My thesis is that in order to restore the balance of our civilization, in order to adjust our social, economic and political life to the violent changes which physical science has directly and indirectly produced, we need to have far more knowledge (systematically ordered scientific knowledge) of human nature and of the life of society than we yet have."

Despite the fact that science is indissolubly bound up with the multifarious techniques of civilised life, it cannot be denied that the organisation of civilised life *as a unified whole* is more haphazard and governed by expediency than it is scientific. By almost common consent it is ruled inadmissible that science, applied so successfully in our control of material nature, should have anything to say in our frantic efforts to control human nature. Why is it that science and politics have, in practice, so little in common when, from a practical point of view, they have complementary and mutually interpenetrating objects? Politics is the technique of government, of control of human society; science, in its wider sense, is the technique by which human beings master or control their environment. Is not human society part of the human environment? Why then do we keep science and politics in two independent and watertight compartments? Have they really nothing whatever to say about each other?

The widespread, almost universal, assumption is that the general settlement of social problems is purely a question of political opinion or of "practical" politics; on in which science, as such, has and can have no direct part and no say. In the, past scientific and literary men have contributed in no small measure to the maintenance of this attitude by a frequently expressed prejudice that the subject-matter of politics is forever outside the scope of scientific method. It is a long established idea among scientists that it is not the business of science to say how its results shall be socially applied; that the limits of its social uses are solely the responsibility of the layman. Science must not "meddle in politics." For instance, in his contribution to *Science and the Changing World*, Sir Oliver Lodge says: "(Machines) are made possible by science, but the responsibility for their use or abuse belongs not to science but to civilisation. If so-called civilisation allows machinery to sap human freedom and enslave mankind, science washes its hands of any such egregious folly." In recent times, it is true, there has been some awakening on the part of a number – a minority – of scientists and scientific writers, who have urged that science cannot, consistent with its own aims and the best interests of its development, stand by disinterested and aloof from politics. Probably three main external influences have converged to help produce this change. One was the rise of communism in Russia and another the rise of fascism. The sharp contrast provided by Soviet Russia and Nazi Germany in their respective treatments of science and scientists, undoubtedly did much to undermine the conception of a "neutral" science aloof and untouched by political struggles. It showed that, if science is disinterested in the trend of politics, at any rate politics is not disinterested in the trend and fate of science. It showed, in short, that science cannot remain always unaffected by what happens in the political sphere. The third factor was the approach and onset of the Second World War, when science was once again to be put in harness and exploited to the full for the mass destruction of life and property.

The result of these and other influences has been an outcrop of books and pamphlets over a period of the last few years, dealing with the status of science in society – its social function, attitude, frustrations, relations and so forth. Yet, despite these evidences of a growing conviction that science cannot continue altogether outside the sphere of politics, neutral and indifferent to the manner in which its discoveries are applied, the rigid division customarily drawn between the two fields and their mutual exclusiveness in practice, still remain.

In view of the foregoing it would seem pertinent to consider the following question: in what manner and to what extent can science, with any benefit to mankind, enter the domain of politics? After all, it is not much use to assert that science must drop its impartiality and quit being indifferent to the political scene, if nothing is forthcoming to indicate what sort of positive action is to be taken in the matter.

Unfortunately, any implications of a practical kind, in most of the literature dealing with the problem of science and society, appear to be either somewhat obscure or entirely lacking. While most of these writers seem generally agreed on the type of economic changes which are necessary for a more scientifically organised society, they give no indication of how science can help in bringing these economic changes about. That is to say, science can assist the necessary economic and technological reorganisation but it must remain dumb on practical political matters and political theory, on, how this reorganisation can actually be politically effected. The scientifically-minded are merely left to take sides in the chaos of unscientific, controversial political theories, techniques and tactics which characterises modern political life. Thus, in practice, science as such is still effectively barred from participation in politics. There is certainly no evidence of an organised and coherent *political* theory capable of general, or at least wide, acceptance by men of science. Although there may be among them a higher proportion which tends toward the Left, scientists and scientifically-minded people are, on the whole, almost as divided as the layman when it comes to political theory.

Useful as it is to draw notice to a problem, the time must come when this is not enough. Writers are usually still content to dwell at great length on the negative aspects of the question; that is, they concentrate mainly on drawing attention to the existing social conditions as they relate to, restrict and canalise the development of science and its technological applications. They declare or (more often) imply that the removal of these conditions will allow the full or better utilisation of scientific discovery for the benefit of the whole community. But again little or nothing is said about how those conditions are to be or can be changed. Whatever their respective views may be on this most important topic they are usually left undeclared, though sometimes, the writers concerned assert that this matter can safely be left to the growing understanding and intelligence of the non-scientific masses! As scientists or writers on science, they cannot openly avow their political convictions presumably for fear of compromising their scientific objectivity.

This reluctance to step boldly into the political scene, on the part of those who reject the notion of a neutral science, only serves to underline the lack of science in politics and the crying need for scientific political theory.

If the scientific taboo on politics and the political taboo on science can be broken down at all, if this social barrier between the two can be removed and the way paved towards a scientific control of human society, then – the present writer is firmly convinced – it can only come from a sound theoretical development and application of scientific method to the political subject-matter: that is, to man's social consciousness. On this view the penetration must be mutual. Science can only become political in so far as politics becomes scientific. It cannot be a one-sided affair; science cannot enter politics with political theory remaining in its present controversial and anarchical condition.

Here, then, when we contemplate the general dearth of scientific understanding of political phenomena and the prevailing ignorance of the laws of political development, we are approaching the main source of the present social barrier between these two great fields of human activity – fields which, as I think can dearly be shown, while formerly so distinct, contain per se no underlying, irreconcilable difference, but rather, are so fundamentally and essentially the same, they are truly but one field with two broad subdivisions.

Meanwhile, in the intervals of peace, with poverty and unemployment on every hand, much-needed wealth is produced only to be destroyed in order to maintain or raise market prices. The abundance, made possible by science, cannot be sold and used. More and more producers are dismissed their jobs and markets contract still further. The unsold wealth goes on piling up while, faced by a dwindling home market, the industrialists of each nation exert pressure upon their governments in the vain endeavour to increase or maintain their exports. Then, in the feverish and desperate struggle for markets at all costs, the governments of the nations come into conflict with one another over technical questions of territory, minorities, resources, colonies, raw materials etc., etc. This conflict eventually leads to open warfare – and, in these days, to modern world war with its mass slaughter and destruction on an ever-increasing scale. "Germany must export" cried Hitler before the Second World War, "or die!"

1.2 The Political Groups

Is there no solution to this paradoxical and catastrophic state of affairs – for which science is partly, if indirectly, responsible? Or is there a way out? In modern times there has been a tendency for this question to form the background of a great deal of political thought and controversy. As this political strife is closely connected with our paradox, with the periodic social upheavals of world war and with socio-economic forces which threaten the possible disruption of civilised society, it may pay us to direct our attention for a while to the ideological aspect of the problem – an aspect which has been rather neglected.

On the whole political opinion is divided on the issues of our paradox as between Right and Left: on the one hand, the extreme Right-wing maintaining the inevitability of the paradox – placing the responsibility for it upon the permanent, incorrigible irrationality and avariciousness of human nature – and, on the other hand, the extreme Left-wing, having a much greater faith in human nature – presuming mankind as a whole capable of rationality – demanding the complete elimination of the paradox by the abolition of its economic basis, i.e., the system of private ownership of the means of social production. Mostly all other opinion falls in between these two extremes.

Let us briefly examine this broadly graded scale of political opinion.

The first thing we note, by observing the relevant evidence of world political history[1] [See table page 25] and records for the last hundred years or so, up to the present time (roughly the duration of the growth of modern capitalism and political democracy) is that one end of the scale – which we will call the "lower" end – is associated with:

> (a) that section of opinion which regards economic individualism, private enterprise and initiative in industry, and private ownership of the means of life, as inevitable, necessary or desirable – and which is opposed, either implicitly or explicitly, to the idea of common

---

[1] Despite the fact that the socialist, communist and anarchist theories were formulated and disseminated in their modern forms nearly a century ago by Marx (b. 1818), Engels (b. 1820), Proudhon (b. 1809), Bakunin (b. 1814), Kropotkin (b. 1842) – with older forms of socialism, even earlier, by Saint-Simon (b. 1760) and Fourier (b. 1772) – despite this, in no country anywhere in the world, so far, has there ever been a government (elected on the basis of universal suffrage and free choice of political party – the multi-party system) with a mandate for carrying out the fundamental principles of any of these theories. It would, of course, need a succession of such freely-elected governments to provide incontrovertible evidence that the mass of people can be, with any degree of permanence, identified with economic collectivism. *Whitaker's Almanack* (1945) gives the following parliamentary majorities for Great Britain from 1833. It should be noted that (a) though the Labour Party gained a majority of seats at the 1945 General Election, the vote they secured represented but a minority of the total electorate, (b) the Labour Party had no mandate from its electors to transform the system of private ownership into that of common ownership.

22

ownership and its implications;
(b) the vast majority of people.

The necessary corollary of this condition is that the other end of the scale – which we will call the "higher," end – is associated with:

(c) that section of opinion which regards a classless, stateless, social system (based on common ownership and democratic control of social production) as inevitable, necessary or desirable, and which is explicitly opposed to the present system of private ownership;
(d) a small minority of people.

In between these two extremes we have, represented on the scale, various sections of opinion which, broadly speaking, constitute a series of modifications such that:

(e) the extreme sections of opinion tend to shade into one another towards the centre of the scale;
(f) the inverse-ratio relationship is preserved generally throughout between 'height' in the scale, of any section of opinion, and the numerical support it commands.

We can thus liken our scale, as a first approximation, to a kind of cone or pyramid. Actually it can be more accurately represented by a hyperbolic curve. Here, however, for the sake of simplicity, we can conveniently and graphically represent our scale of opinion by drawing a vertical section through the apex of our supposed cone or pyramid as in Fig. 1. It will appear as a triangle.

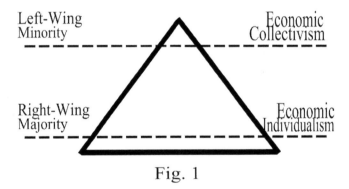

Fig. 1

We have used the terms "economic collectivism" and "economic individualism" in the diagram quite advisedly, in order to distinguish this type from another type of collectivism and individualism, which, we shall presently go on to consider. This other type is indicated by the terms "political collectivism" and "political individualism."

By placing the extreme Left-wing minority at or near the apex of the triangle we have put them "higher" in the scale of political opinion – in other words, we have implied that they are "Intellectuals." Likewise, by placing the extreme Right-wing majority near the base of the triangle, we have put them "lower" in the scale; and we shall find it convenient to use the term "masses" – i.e., non-intellectuals – to designate those who occupy the lowest level in the political scale.

In case our use of these two latter terms, "intellectuals" and "masses," is called into question, let us at once admit that we are using them in rather restricted senses. Yet, as we shall clearly show later on, our use of them in these connections is fully justified. In the first place we must sharply distinguish between "intellect" and "intelligence." The dictionary and common usage do not make any clear-cut distinction between these two words whereas science must and does. Psychologists have shown that intelligence is largely and predominantly inborn, or inherited, and that it remains fairly constant throughout the major part of a person's life. Our own work, on the other hand, tends to show that intellect is intimately connected with ideology, that it is, in fact, largely a function of the ideological development of an individual, and that a person's intellect may change enormously during his or her lifetime.

Environmental influence plays a great part in determining intellect and intellectual growth, whereas this is not the case with intelligence, which can be developed hardly at all and is little influenced by environment and education. While making this sharp distinction between intellect and intelligence it must not be thought that we assume them to have no connection and to be entirely unrelated to one another. Our differentiation between these two terms serves merely to show that our scale of political opinion or beliefs is not a measure of *intelligence*, and that a great degree of intelligence can be manifested in people who occupy a low level of intellectual development, and contrariwise, a moderate degree of intelligence can be manifested in people who occupy a high level of intellectual development. Thus the term "masses" does not *necessarily* exclude persons of the greatest intelligence though, for reasons which will become apparent in due course, it may be uncommon for such people to occupy the lowest *intellectual* level for very long.

What we do suggest, however, is that our scale of political outlooks has a direct and close relationship with the growth of intellect, or rather, with an *aspect* of intellectual development – and the most important and significant aspect at that, namely: the *qualitative* development of intellect. To many this will no doubt seem a bold and altogether gratuitous suggestion, incapable of standing up to scrutiny or of bearing any real examination. Nevertheless – and notwithstanding the ideological prejudices that such a suggestion is likely to call forth – it is one of our aims to transform the suggestion and establish it, beyond all reasonable scepticism, as a fact.

The question will most certainly occur as to what we mean by *qualitative* development of intellect. We use the term in order to distinguish this aspect of intellectual growth from the *quantitative* aspect of its development. In explanation, it will suffice for present purposes to remind the reader of the distinction, recognised by common thought and everyday language, between "deep" knowledge and "wide" knowledge. The intellect, in other words, develops in two ways: (1) *vertically* ("deep") or qualitatively, and (2) *horizontally* ("wide") or quantitatively. Most of us, at some time or another, have come across people who seem to have almost encyclopaedic knowledge – that is to say, people who have a great *quantity* of factual information at their disposal – yet who, despite their very "wide" range of knowledge, have no "deep" insight or understanding into the nature of things, and of the facts with which they are so liberal. Such persons are unable to bring "widely" separated facts and classes of fact into "deep" relation with one another; they are unable to make the "deep" generalisations so necessary for the "highest" development of intellect. Of such people it is often remarked that they have "shallow" minds or that they "know so much but understand so little."

Conversely, of course, we have that type of person – also to be met with – whose knowledge, whilst "narrow" in scope or extent, is yet "deep" and "highly" generalised. And in between the two extreme types all kinds of combinations, involving every degree of these aspects (of vertical and horizontal development) are theoretically possible in the mental organisation of people. When these concepts become more familiar and determinate we shall be able to see how, quite often, "distinguished" or "brilliant" people, persons of "refinement and culture" or people belonging to the "educated" and "upper" classes are people with no more than a low vertical development of intellect but who have a fair or generous horizontal development plus a fair or large degree of intelligence (which, as we saw, is largely inborn). Thus, such individuals, so far as they concern our scale of opinion – which we suggest is also a scale of qualitative or vertical intellectual growth – belong to the lower levels of the scale, some, possibly, to the lowest: to what we have called the "masses."

So we see that the use to which we shall put the terms "intellectuals" and "masses" is not quite the same, and should be clearly distinguished from, the more vague and indefinite senses of normal, everyday use.

Especially should we be very clear about this, as the common usage of the terms approximates, somewhat, to our ideological sense. For example, the term "masses," as ordinarily used frequently means "the lower orders" i.e., the most numerous and poorest section *in the economic or social scale*. The *Concise Oxford Dictionary* (1944) gives, under the heading "class," the following: "*the classes, the rich or educated, as opposed to *the masses*.*" Hence a rich person, educated or not, cannot belong to the masses – and an "educated" person, rich or not, also cannot be included. The ideological sense in which we shall use the term does away with this ambiguity and vagueness and gives it a more precise meaning. If we were to make a comparison between our ideological scale of opinion and a similar scale, showing the numbers of people who occupy different levels in the economic or income hierarchy, we should find that, at their bases, both scales would have in common the majority of those who occupy the lowest levels of each, but, as we ascend to the upper levels of both scales We should find this community of membership becoming progressively less until at the topmost levels we should find few or no members at all in common. The two scales would be divergent in this respect.

Year	Party	Majority
1833	Whig	307
1835	Whig	107
1837	Whig	51
1841	Cons.	81
1847	Whig	1
1852	Lib.	13
1857	Lib.	79
1859	Lib.	43
1868	Lib.	128
1874	Cons.	46
1880	Lib.	62
1885	Lib. and Nat.	166
1886	Unionist	114
1892	Lib.	40
1895	Unionist	152
1900	Unionist	134
1906	Lib.	356
1910	Lib.	124
1910	Lib.	126
1918	Coalit.	263
1922	Cons.	79
1923	No majority	
1924	Cons.	225
1929	No majority	
1931	Nat. Govt.	425
1935	Nat. Govt.	247

1.3 The Left Wing and Intellectualism

WITH regard to our contention that the Left-wing political outlook represents, or is indicative of, a higher qualitative level of intellectual development than the Right-wing outlook; we might, perhaps, have been forgiven for expecting a clear recognition of its truth on the part of those who actually occupy these higher levels. Yet, curiously enough, when we come to examine the voluminous theoretical writings and extensive literature which issues almost continuously from Left-wing sources, we rarely, if ever, find any explicit recognition of this. Though the proposition may be implied in a great deal of their writings, that it does not – or rarely does – find expression in any explicitly conscious form, is, in itself, a truly remarkable fact. One would think that, if they were fully aware of their intellectual relationship with the Right-wing, they would make the utmost use of the knowledge and turn it to good account as a possible weapon in their political struggles with the Right. The fact that as a political weapon it would probably have little or no effect on the unintellectual masses does not explain the matter for, as the history of the Left movement shows, they have no hesitation in using their more theoretical ideas as propaganda – with the usual consequence that they fail to attract any positive interest or support for them from the vast majority of those to whom they appeal. And as this absence of explicit reference to their general intellectual superiority is hardly likely to be due to sheer modesty, we must begin to suspect that they are not fully and consciously aware of their real relationship in this respect. We shall soon see that our suspicions are largely justified.

We must be very careful, however, not to convey the impression that we think them grossly or wholly unaware of *the fact* of their intellectual superiority. Doubtless, most members of the extreme Left-wing groups already take it for granted (at least in the political sphere). They themselves refer to "the ignorance of the masses," of "the mental bankruptcy of the Right." They exhort the masses to "think for themselves," to "use their own reason" and speak of "the task of educating the masses." Nevertheless, what we do suggest, for reasons which will become evident, is that these members of the Left are not aware of the true position – that, indeed, they have no clear conception *of a vertical or qualitative intellectual development of a general and universal nature, the various levels of which are directly related to all existing and possible political outlooks.* The *explicit* acceptance, or *conscious* assumption, of intellectual superiority in this or that particular sphere (which is common to all outlooks) is a very different thing from the scientific or rational demonstration, from empirically ascertained facts, of the direct connection of political standpoints as a whole with a *general* development of the intellect, and the relative positions occupied therein by the Right and Left. It is these latter we propose to undertake as part of the establishment and development of our main thesis. That members of the Left tend to cling to the more vulgar notion of intellectual growth (as a mere quantitative accumulation of factual knowledge in this or that particular field) is indicated by their references to "political knowledge," "political consciousness," "political maturity," "socialist understanding," "communist consciousness" – as though these were largely independent of a general or qualitative development of intellect.

When we turn to the literature and speeches of the opponents of the Left, we find, surprisingly enough, quite a considerable amount of corroboration – implied in many tacit admissions that the Left-wing is intellectual – of our thesis regarding the close relationship between outlook or ideology and vertical intellectual development. Here, for instance, are a few examples of this admission.

In his book *A False Utopia: Collectivism in Theory and Practice*, published by the Right Book Club (1937), the conservative William Henry Chamberlain writes:

> The Soviet Constitution defines the membership of the Communist Party as consisting of 'the most active and politically conscious citizens.' The idea of a state ruled by a model intellectual elite has found its champions from Plato to H. G. Wells. As a relief from the imperfections, compromises, and disillusionments that followed the general adoption of democratic institutions during the nineteenth century its appeal is obvious. Serious difficulties, however, crop up when the question arises how the select minority is to be chosen. (p. 38.)

However – as a result of his confusion of communism with fascism, a common error – he contradicts himself a few pages further on by including the Soviet Union in his characterization of fascism as definitely anti-intellectual:

> The modern-style dictatorship is definitely and implacably anti-intellectual. Whether it is Goebbels in Germany or Kaganovitch in the Soviet Union, or some lieutenant of Mussolini in Italy, a favourite theme of communist-fascist oratory is the contrast between the splendid discipline of the workers and peasants in supporting the existing regime and the contemptible surreptitious grumbling of the intellectuals. It is an ironical commentary on the naive enthusiasm of a certain type of left-wing intellectual in Western Europe and America for Russian communism in theory and practice that the Soviet Union has shot, jailed, and driven into exile a higher proportion of its educated class than any other country in the world. (p. 46.)

The last sentence in the above quotation contains a good example of the common habit of confounding – as a consequence of the inability to distinguish vertical with horizontal intellectual development. Chamberlain continues:

> But Stalin, Hitler and Mussolini are psychologically quite correct when they see in the intellectual who thinks for himself and even, on occasion, feels a moral obligation to express some critical idea, the deadliest menace to their systems. What these systems, which rely for their existence on mass emotional stimulation plus terrorism, naturally fear above everything else is cool rational criticism, sober deflation of their self-magnified achievements. Hence there must be war to the death on the independent intelligentsia. (p. 48.)

Elsewhere he distinguishes between the Left-wing and fascism and, incidentally, in so doing shows once again his association of the Left-wing with intellectualism:

> One mildly disquieting symptom is the defeatist attitude toward individual liberty and the democratic methods of government that

is prevalent in some circles of the left-wing intelligentsia in Great Britain and America. Intellectual advocacy of fascism is still a rarity... (p. 242.)

Another typical example of the intellectual Left-wing identification is furnished by Sir R. M. Banks in his *The Conservative Outlook* (1929):

I prefer the phrase 'characteristics and ideals' to the word 'principles' for the Tory mind has always had a distaste for those abstract principles so dear to the Jacobin, the Radical, the Socialist and the Communist. 'The Rights of Man,' 'Democratic Ideas,' 'Abstract Justice,' 'Social Contracts,' all the stock-in-trade of the encyclopaedist and the doctrinaire, are to the Tory mind dangerous idols upon whose altars the happiness of peoples has been sacrificed over and over again. (p. 7.) Respect for continuity and authority; loyalty to national institutions, especially the national Crown, the national Church, and the national ties within the Empire; a belief in private property of every kind as the best basis for the State; a preference for the practical as opposed to the theoretic... (p. 16.)

Again, Lord Hugh Cecil commences the first chapter of his well-known book *Conservatism* with the following:

Natural conservatism is a tendency of the human mind. It is a disposition averse from change; and it springs partly from a distrust of the unknown and a corresponding reliance on experience rather than on theoretic reasoning; partly from a faculty in men to adapt themselves to their surroundings so that what is familiar merely because of its familiarity becomes more acceptable or more tolerable than what is unfamiliar. Distrust of the unknown, and preference for experience over theory, are deeply seated in almost all minds and are expressed in often quoted proverbs: 'Look before you leap,' 'A bird in hand is worth two in the bush,' 'An ounce of fact is worth a pound of theory' – these are sayings that express a well-nigh universal conservative sentiment. (p. 9.)

We see the same views expressed by the Right even as far back as Disraeli:

In a progressive country change is constant; and the great question is not whether you should resist change, which is inevitable, but whether that change should be carried out in deference to the manners, the customs, the laws, the traditions of the people, or in deference to abstract principles and arbitrary and general doctrines. (Speech quoted with approval by Winston Churchill in his 1945 New Year message to the Primrose League.)

More modern is the following (from Colm Brogan's *Who are 'the People'?* 1943):

Progressive 'intellectuals,' journalists and political leaders speak for The People, pleading their cause against the arrogant stupidity of the ruling classes. How the rulers managed to survive the fervour of the attack and the consequences of their own incompetence must be a mystery to every student of progressive literature. The rulers have almost every fault that can be ascribed to humanity, but, somehow,

> they hang on; they keep their powers and authority. Obviously,
> they know something. What they know is hard to discover and is
> certainly unfair, but it is technically important. Twice the Labour
> Party has formed a Government and twice it has fallen out of the
> seat of power as if it were a hammock. There is some trick about
> keeping in which Labour has not quite grasped, and, indeed, may
> never grasp. For Labour is not The People. In many respects,
> Labour positively misrepresents The People. (p. 2.)

An even more recent example is to be found in Mr. Winston Churchill's second
(1945) election speech over the radio:

> Both at home and abroad there is a full four years' work for all to
> do. That is the reason why I have censured in the most severe terms
> the Socialist effort to drag their long-term fads and wavy Utopias
> across the practical path of need and duty...
>
> There could never be a worse time to raise these academic
> Socialist arguments than now, when all the practical tasks which
> stare us in the face, and upon which we are engaged, would be
> delayed, confused, interrupted and perhaps stricken to the ground.
> (Reported by *Daily Telegraph*, 14-6-45.)

Besides this tacit tendency of the Right to regard the Left-wing as intellectual we
should note well that it goes hand in hand with a certain anti-intellectualism and
hostility, or scepticism, directed against the characteristic features of the intellectual
outlook: i.e., doctrine, theory, logic, reason, generalisation, abstract principle and
academic discussion etc.

Moreover, it is to the extreme Right-wing – viz. fascism – that we have to turn
for the most extreme examples of anti-intellectualism (wherein we can still detect
the underlying implication which identifies intellectualism with the Left).

Among the quotations given in Professor N. Gangulee's interesting anthology of
pronouncements from official Nazi sources (*The Mind and Face of Nazi Germany*)
are these:

> In my *Ordensburgen* a youth will grow up before which the world
> will shrink back. A violently active, dominating, intrepid, brutal
> youth – that is what I am after. Youth must be all those things.
> It must be indifferent to pain. There must be no weakness or
> tenderness in it. I want to see once more in its eyes the gleam of
> pride and independence of the beast of prey. Strong and handsome
> must my young men be. I will have them fully trained in all physical
> exercises. I intend to have an athletic youth – that is the first and
> chief thing. In this way I shall eradicate the thousands of years
> of human domestication. Then I shall have in front of me the
> pure and noble natural material. With that I can create the new
> order. I will have no intellectual training. Knowledge is ruin to my
> young men... (Hitler to Rauschning, p. 172.) Germany today is a
> National-Socialist state. The ideology by which we are governed
> is diametrically opposed to that of Soviet Russia... We National
> Socialists recognise that every people has the right to its own inner
> life according to its own needs and character. Bolshevism, on the

other hand, lays down doctrinaire theories, to be accepted by all nations without regard to their particular qualities, talents, etc.... Bolshevism fights for a theory and sacrifices for it millions of human beings, destroys incalculable cultural and traditional values, and achieves, in comparison with us, only a very low standard of living for all... (Hitler, Reichstag speech, 1935. pp. 154-5)

Humanity, the all-embracing Church and the sovereign individual who have freed themselves from blood ties, no longer represent to us absolute values, but doubtful or even perishing dogmas. They lack polarity and represent a violation of nature for the sake of mere abstractions... In the prehistoric ages man follows the blood demands in life and cult as in a dream... Later... in the process of civilisation, he becomes more and more intellectual. This leads finally not to creative conflicts but to division. Thus, reason turns away from race and species. The individual detached from the ties of blood and from the sequence of the generations, falls a victim to absolute abstractions... and mixes with alien blood. The result of this incest is the death of personality, nation, race and civilisation. (Alfred Rosenberg, pp. 109-10)

Discussion of matters affecting our existence and that of the nation must cease altogether. Anyone who dares to question the rightness of the National-Socialist outlook will be branded as a traitor. (Sauckel, Governor of Thuringia, 1933. p. 116.)

We can see no flaw in the Fuhrer's reasoning: difficulties? yes; doubts? yes; alternatives? none. What we want today is unity. Where did the intellectuals lead us? Into a barren wilderness where was neither hope nor love of each other or our country or race; and without these what is there in life? (A Nazi youth to Sir Arnold Wilson, 1934. p. 126.)

In an article contributed by Mussolini in 1932 to the fourteenth volume of *Enciclopedia Italiana*, he declares:

When... I summoned a meeting at Milan... I had no specific doctrinal attitude in my mind. I had experience of one doctrine only – that of Socialism, from 1903-4 to the winter of 1914 – that is to say about a decade: and from Socialism itself, even though I had taken part in the movement first as a member of the rank and file and then later as a leader, yet I had no experience of its doctrine in practice. My own doctrine, even in this period, had always been a doctrine of action. A unanimous, universally-accepted theory of Socialism did not exist after 1905, when the revisionist movement began in Germany under the leadership of Bernstein... Fascism was not the nurseling of a doctrine worked out beforehand with detailed elaboration; it was born of the need for action and was itself from the beginning practical rather than theoretical... (pp. 7-8, *The Political and Social Doctrine of Fascism*: Hogarth Press.)

Giovanni Gentile, "appointed to a place in Mussolini's Ministry after the 'March on Rome' and prime mover of that scholastic reform which Mussolini, described as the 'most Fascist of all Fascist reforms'," affirmed in a speech at Palermo, March 1924:

> ... I am very much inclined to believe that the true doctrine is that which does not express itself in typed words, but in the actions and personalities of its exponents... Let us quit books, then, and consider the spirit of the deeds which throughout history have meant so much more to us than any expounded doctrines... (quoted by Giuseppe Prezzolini in his *Fascism* pp. 98-9)

During the Spanish Civil War, the "great Catholic writer and philosopher," Miguel Unamuno – who, at its beginning, favoured the fascist cause as against the "Reds" – was horrified at the brutalities ordered by the fascist General Staff. He wrote:

> All these crimes are committed in cold blood, in response to the slogan implied by the double-edged cry of this insane general who calls himself Millan Astray: 'Death to intelligence and long live death!' (quoted by Melvin Rader in *No Compromise* p. 136)

A further example is afforded by Dr. Kahrstedt, Professor of History at Gottingen University, in a speech given on Empire Day in Nazi Germany:

> We renounce international science. We renounce the international republic of learning. We renounce research for its own sake. (*Nature* 18-1-36)

James Drennan, supporter of fascism generally and writer for the British Union of Fascists declares in his *B.U.F.: Oswald Mosley and British Fascism*:

> Fascism arose, then, out of the din of unrecorded street-fights and the mess of factory brawls and the quick butchery of country-side ambushes, and emerged as a direct and violent will-to-power. The democrats met the movement with the laughable legend that these grim and wild young men were nothing more than the hired hooligan bands of 'the capitalists.' The explanation was characteristic of the democratic mind, but it hardly accounts for the dynamic surge of armed manhood in no time out of nowhere... The Liberals are also puzzled by the *lack of theory* in Fascism... Fascism has no long pedigree of theory, like Socialism, Liberalism and Communism and other products of the intellectual laboratory. Fascism is real insurrection – an insurrection of *feeling* – a mutiny of *men* against the conditions of the modern world. It is completely characteristic of this aspect of Fascism in its early stages, both in Italy and in Germany, that the movement should have grown to full strength without either logical theory behind it, or cut-and-dried programme in front of it. The men who have built Fascism in Italy and Germany – who are the 'common men,' the 'men in the street,' leave theories to the intellectuals and programmes to the democrats who have betrayed them with programmes for a century. The Fascist is concerned with the problem of power, and he aims at the achievement of power through action... He acts, in fact, instinctively, and not theoretically. The opposition between Fascism and Social Democracy is the opposition between life and theory, between man and intellect, between blood and paper. (pp. 211-3)

In his excellent and well-documented book on fascism, *No Compromise*, Melvin Rader writes of "one of the main aspects of Fascist anti-intellectualism: the refusal to employ science in the determination of basic human ideals." He goes on to describe the strong influence of "that forerunner of Fascism, Vilfredo Pareto" upon Mussolini and his sympathisers: "His (Mussolini's) remarks indicate that he was especially impressed by Pareto's denial of the intellectual, political, religious and moral unity of society... The Fascists either leave no room for pure theory, or subordinate it to morale and action. Typical of the Fascist attitude are the words of an early Nazi theorist, Moeller van den Bruck: 'The future belongs not to the problem-monger, but to the man of character'... in the *Popolo d'Italia*, November 22, 1921, Mussolini himself champions the relativistic position. Endeavouring to go the relativists one better, he defines Fascism as 'super-relativity.' The Fascists, he asserts, display their extremely relativistic outlook by refusing to give a definite form to their programme and by recognising 'in life and action an absolute supremacy over intelligence.'"

Has the strong anti-intellectual, anti-rational bias of the Right-wing – and particularly that of fascism – nothing to do with their vehement opposition to the Left? Is it mere coincidence or is there, as we suggest, a very intimate connection between the two? Is there not really an implicit recognition of the identity of the Left-wing ideology with a higher level of intellectual development than their own? Is not implied here our present thesis that there is a direct relationship between political outlooks or ideologies, on the one hand, and the vertical or qualitative development of intellect, on the other? What, we suggest, is here merely implicit, we shall, in due course, confirm with much stronger evidence in its favour.

1.4 The Masses and Emotional Suggestibility

H AVING made out a more or less *prima facie* case for the possibility of the connection between political outlook and vertical growth of intellect, we shall now proceed to follow up the suggestion and turn our attention to a very general survey, or bird's-eye view, of those aspects of intellectualism and its development which relate particularly to our original scale of political opinion (Fig. 1).

In this scale we noted a whole series of political outlooks as they relate to, and are identified with, two basic forms of the economic structure of society, i.e., (1), economic individualism (private ownership and control of means of production) and (2), economic collectivism (common ownership and control of means of production). We also noticed that the extreme ends of the scale (the apex and the base) represent the more purist types of outlook; that is to say, they represent those outlooks which (a), tend to lay great stress on, or identify themselves wholly with, one or the other of the two basic economic forms and (b), tend to ignore or wholly reject the economic form complementary to that with which they are identified.

Again, we noted that the middle sections of opinion (some of which call themselves and are known as "moderate") represent modifications of, or compromises between, these two extremes. We saw too that from the available evidence up to the present time, a larger number of people tend to support the lower extreme (economic individualism) than any other level, and that the numerical support for the various levels progressively diminishes as we ascend from the lower extreme to the upper (economic collectivism).

Let us begin our broad survey of the political aspects of intellectualism by examining and comparing the most general intellectual characteristics of these various levels. We will start with the lowest and most numerous level: the masses.

If we consider almost any large gathering of people, especially of the casual or more unorganised kind – such as the kind which congregates in the street, in the cinema, or at a football match – or, again, if we take an equally large but dispersed number of people at complete random, then it will follow, from what has been said above regarding the numerical representation of the different levels, that on the whole, in such groups, people who occupy the lowest level will largely preponderate. On an average – and assuming those of the higher levels go to the cinema, football matches, dog-racing etc., as frequently as do those of the lower levels, which, to say the least, is doubtful – such large gatherings of people will exhibit a political structure similar to, or approximating, that of our scale. (If there is any difference it is most likely to be an increase in the numerical proportion of the lower levels.)

Now, random or casual groups and crowds of this unorganised kind have been made the subject of study by eminent psychologists and other students and writers.

What strikes one forcibly when reading and comparing the results of their inquiries is the fact that all, almost without exception, place great stress on these two dominating and complementary characteristics of such groups: (a), the patent lack of intellectuality and (b), the high degree of mass emotional suggestibility or contagion of feeling.

For instance, Gustave Le Bon, in his well-known book *The Crowd: A Study of the Popular Mind*, emphasises the "extreme mental inferiority of crowds" and states that they are given to great emotionalism, suggestibility, and the inability to reason or to adopt an objective, rational, independent attitude. The average crowd, maintains Le Bon, is pre-eminently destructive and negative in character; it, worships the aggressive strong man, the dictator, and abases itself before him.

Again, in his interesting and more scientific study, *The Group Mind*, William McDougall says much the same thing. The unorganised type of group is "excessively emotional, impulsive, violent, fickle, inconsistent, irresolute and extreme in action, displaying only the coarser emotions and the less refined sentiments; extremely suggestible, careless in deliberation, hasty in judgment, incapable of any but the simpler and imperfect forms of reasoning; easily swayed and led, lacking in self-consciousness, devoid of self-respect and of sense of responsibility; and apt to be carried away by the consciousness of its own force, so that it tends to produce all the manifestations we have learnt to expect of any irresponsible and absolute power. Hence its behaviour is like that of any unruly child or an untutored passionate savage in a strange situation... "

Freud, in his *Group Psychology and the Analysis of the Ego*, affirms, "Thus the group appears to us as a revival of the primal horde. Just as primitive man virtually survives in every individual, so the primal horde may arise once more out of any random crowd; in so far as men are habitually under the sway of group formation we recognise in it the survival of the primal horde. We must conclude that the psychology of the group is the oldest psychology; what we have isolated as individual psychology, by neglecting all traces of the group, has only since come into prominence out of the old group psychology by a gradual process which may still, perhaps, be described as incomplete."

In this excellent and original study Freud refers extensively to the work of Le Bon and that of McDougall and quotes them with approval at some length: "... the individual forming part of a group acquires solely from numerical considerations, a sentiment of invincible power which allows him to yield to instincts which, had he been alone he would perforce have kept under restraint. He will be the less disposed to check himself from the consideration that, a group being anonymous, and in consequence irresponsible, the sentiment of responsibility which always controls individuals disappears entirely... " (quoting Le Bon.

Still referring to Le Bon, Freud continues:

> Inclined as it is to all extremes, a group can only be excited by an excessive stimulus. Anyone who wishes to produce an effect upon it needs no logical adjustment in his arguments: he must paint in the most forcible colours, he must exaggerate, and he must repeat the same thing again and again...
>
> Since a group is in no doubt as to what constitutes truth or error, and is conscious, moreover, of its own great strength, it is as intolerant as it is obedient to authority. It respects force and can only be slightly influenced by kindness, which it regards merely as a form of weakness. What it demands of its heroes is strength, or even violence. It wants to be ruled and oppressed and to fear its masters. Fundamentally it is entirely conservative, and it has a deep aversion from all innovations and advances and an unbounded

respect for tradition...

Some other features in Le Bon's description show in a clear light how well justified is the identification of the group mind with the mind of primitive people. In groups the most contradictory ideas can exist side by side and tolerate each other, without any conflict arising from the logical contradiction between them. But this is also the case in the unconscious mental life of individuals, of children and of neurotics, as psychoanalysis has long pointed out...

The manner in which individuals are thus carried away by a common impulse is explained by McDougall by means of what he calls the 'principle of direct induction of emotion by way of the primitive sympathetic response' (p. 25), that is, by means of the emotional contagion with which we are all familiar. The fact is that the perception of the signs of an emotional state is calculated automatically to arouse the same emotion in the person who perceives them. The greater the number of people in whom the same emotion can be simultaneously observed, the stronger does this automatic compulsion grow. The individual loses his power of criticism, and lets himself slip into the same emotion. But in so doing he increases the excitement of the other people, who had produced this effect upon him; and thus the emotional charge of the individuals becomes intensified by mutual interaction. Something is unmistakably at work in the nature of a compulsion to do the same thing as the others, to remain in harmony with the many. The coarser and simpler emotions are the more apt to spread through a group in this way...

A group impresses the individual with a sense of unlimited power and of insurmountable peril. For the moment it replaces the whole of human society, which is the wielder of authority, whose punishments the individual fears, and for whose sake he has submitted to so many inhibitions. It is clearly perilous for him to put himself in opposition to it, and it will be safer to follow the example of those around him and perhaps even 'hunt with the pack'...

Le Bon traces back all the puzzling features of social phenomena to two factors: the mutual suggestion of individuals and the prestige of leaders. But prestige, again, is only recognisable by its capacity for evoking suggestion. McDougall for a moment gives an impression that his principle of 'primitive induction of emotion' might enable us to do without the assumption of suggestion. But on further consideration we are forced to perceive that this principle says no more than the familiar assertions about 'imitation' or 'contagion,' except for a decided stress on the emotional factor. There is no doubt that something exists in us which, when we become aware of signs of emotion in someone else, tends to make us fall into the same emotion...

I have quoted Freud extensively in his references to Le Bon and McDougall in order to show how unanimous all these writers are in ascribing to the unorganised group, or crowd, a general lack of independent, rational objectivity, on the one hand, and the presence of a large degree of mass or collective emotional suggestibility, on the other.

As a further illustration of these characteristics of random groups we will turn to the work of just one more psychologist, that of Serge Chakotin, pupil of the Russian scientist Pavlov.

In his important study of the psychology of totalitarian political propaganda, *The Rape of the Masses*, Chakotin, in a chapter headed "Collective Psychology," writes:

> A thing that is very characteristic of the crowd, and also, as we shall see, of the masses, is the preponderance of any emotional over any intellectual appeal.

In the same chapter he distinguishes between crowds and masses:

> We have, then, to distinguish between the notions of masses and crowd. A crowd is always a mass, but a mass of individuals is not necessarily a crowd. The mass is generally dispersed; its individuals are not in touch with one another, and psychologically this is an important distinction. In spite of this, there is a bond between the elements of a mass – a certain homogeneity in psychical structure, resulting from close similarity of interests environment, education, nationality, work, and so on. In practice the masses have to be dealt with today more often than the crowd.

Although Chakotin disagrees with the extremism of Le Bon's characterisation of the crowd he nevertheless refers to "the essential reactions of crowds, which, as we have already mentioned, are characterised by Le Bon as resulting from excited sensibilities and from psychical contagion." He goes on: "It is true that a crowd can be aroused to fury and to readiness for violence, and also to delirious enthusiasm; it is true that it is capable of incredible cowardice or sublime heroism. But it is characteristic of it that it acts only under leadership, only when there are protagonists who manipulate it, "soul engineers." Le Bon himself says that "without a leader the crowd is an amorphous being, incapable of action."

The phenomena of lynching might be quoted: it is often sufficient for a single man to make an unconsidered gesture; the contagion will spread to the rest, who will commit any atrocity.

Referring to the phenomenon of suggestion Chakotin says:

> The question of suggestion, especially through the spoken word, or through any symbol, plays an important part here... If we analyse the possibilities of resistance to suggestion – a question, as we shall see, which is of the utmost importance – we find that, apart from pathological cases of congenital inadequacy or sickness or poisoning, these possibilities are largely all function of the degree of culture... which makes up the psychical mechanism of the individuals concerned. Ignorance is thus the best medium for the formation of masses who easily lend themselves to suggestion. This is a capital fact in the domain of politics and the social order... It is often said that consciousness varies inversely with susceptibility to suggestion.

In his book Chakotin relates how an attempt was made, in pre-Nazi Germany, to introduce revolutionary new methods – based on the study of the psychology of groups – into Left-wing and anti-fascist propaganda. The attempt failed, but not because of the ineffectiveness of the new methods. In fact the methods themselves were highly successful; indeed, they were largely the same as the highly successful and new methods of propaganda which were being used by Hitler and his National Socialists, and which played so great a part in promoting the rapid rise of the Nazis to power. The attempt failed because the methods were rejected by the Left-wing leaders, whose doctrinaire attitude branded the new ideas as trifling, unworthy and "dangerous" "... they felt certain objections of principle; they had no great opinion of psychology or of any science of politics." We shall return to this, more fully, later.

Chakotin, for the purposes of conducting propaganda, broadly divides communities into two classes: (1), those who are largely immune to suggestion but who are receptive to theoretical, rational, persuasive arguments and to doctrine; (2), those who are passive, non-intellectual, unobjective or subjective, and greatly susceptible to emotion and suggestion. The relative numerical proportions of these two classes are as 1 to 10 respectively: that is to say, 10 percent are active and thinking, 90 percent passive and emotional. He bases these conclusions partly on an experiment carried out (with anti-fascist propaganda) during election campaigns in Offenbach, Darmstadt, Mainz, Worms, Giessen and Heidelberg in 1932 – an experiment which "was conducted with the rigour of laboratory practice."

We should note, in passing, that Chakotin makes no distinction between vertical and horizontal intellectual development. Hence his 10 percent of active "militants" and thinking people, who resist suggestion, includes an element which, upon our more differentiated analysis, could not be classed as intellectual in the qualitative or vertical sense. This element would embrace both fascist and Right-wing "intellectuals" – i.e., people of low vertical development but who have a comparatively wide horizontal growth – and many of the so-called "educated" people; again, not all "active" and "militant" people are objective, rational or intellectual. This is borne out by Chakotin's references to the followers of the Right-wing and particularly his references to the fact that the Nazis themselves distinguished between the active minority and the passive mass:

> What, then, were the methods of influencing the masses? As we have said, there are two categories of persons; consequently two forms of propaganda were needed, one addressed to the 10 per cent., who are sufficiently sure of themselves to be able to resist crude suggestion, and the other to the passive 90 per cent., who are accessible to suggestion, especially suggestion working on the basis of the first (combative) instinct. This suggestion works by actual menace from time to time, as an absolute factor, and in the interim by the mass dissemination of symbols' which recall the menace and thus act as a conditional factor...These two forms of propaganda, addressed to these two groups of persons, thus differed in principle. The first acted by persuasion, by reasoning; the second by suggestion, by means of fear, now of its positive complement, enthusiasm or excitement, sometimes ecstatic, sometimes furious; these reactions also proceeded from the combative instinct. We call the first of these two forms of propaganda ratio-propaganda and the second senso-propaganda. The first is simply political instruction,

> and needs no lengthy explanation; it is, moreover, the propaganda normally employed by political parties, especially in democratic countries. (pp. 168-9)

And again:

> What is the rational content of propaganda? In the last resort, propaganda has to make use of the psychical levers of which we have spoken in order to influence the passive nine-tenths of mankind, but this has to be done by the remaining tenth, the militants, the thinking and reasoning persons who are immune to emotional propaganda; a rational propaganda is thus also necessary. (Far be it from us to suggest, indeed, that propaganda of. any sort can usefully be carried on with no idea behind it, merely an appropriate technique.) The '10 percent' must be enlightened and guided by some idea... (p. 263)

Chakotin also relates several historical examples of the irrational behaviour typical of crowds as, for instance, the one concerning the invasion by the mob – "filled with hatred of the king" – of the royal palace at Versailles on June 20, 1792. "Yet when the frightened king appeared on the balcony of the palace wearing this *bonnet rouge*, (the red cloth cap of the revolutionary Sansculottes) the crowd at once forgot all else and went into ecstasies at the sight, acclaiming the king with shouts of 'Vive le Roi!'"

1.5 Fear of the Group

WHAT are we to gather from all this evidence from the psychological study of large groups and masses of people?

Firstly, we should note how closely the above descriptions of the psychological characteristics of groups correspond with the characteristics of the fascist outlook – as is evidenced by the quotations, given in Chapter 3, from fascist speakers and writers. (And much of this study of groups, we must remember, was carried on and written about before the advent of fascism or the Nazis.)

The intolerance, violence, logical inconsistency, extremity in action, impulsiveness, irrationalism, docility and servility to absolute authority, respect for force, excessive emotionalism and suggestibility – all these characteristics described by the above-named psychologists as typical of the group, the "mob," are well in accordance with typical and characteristic features of fascism and, as McDougall says, "produce all the manifestations we have learnt to expect of any irresponsible and absolute power." All these characteristics can be found in abundance if we examine fascist utterances and behaviour. Two of the psychologists, we noticed, compare the group to primitive uncivilised man; Freud, in particular, in his *Group Psychology*, endeavours to show an intimate connection between the modern group and the primal horde.

Secondly, but more important, we should note – and note well – the *collective* nature of these characteristic modes of behaviour, thinking and feeling; that is to say, we should clearly observe that they are modes which not only arise out of group formation, but which also lend themselves readily to the formation, and collective expression, of large groups of people, and, moreover, that they are modes which tend to preserve the unity of the group and its behaviour. "Thinking for oneself," "independence of thought," "using one's own reason," "individual judgment," "detached criticism," cannot be expressed by the group as a whole. Indeed, such things presuppose the individual's escape and detachment from the overwhelming mental influence and dictates of the group. And not only is independence of thought incompatible with group or collective expression, but it positively tends to disrupt it and threatens to break up the unity – even the very existence itself – of the group. Hence the intolerance and hostility with which the group meets all attempts, on the part of any individual, to be objective, analytical, theoretical, critical and independent in thought.

Of course, it must be understood that we are referring only to the *majority* of groups and particularly to the larger, the random or more casual kind of group, e.g., gatherings or dispersed associations which are open to and attract the general public.

Nevertheless, much of what we have to say will apply, with suitable modifications, to most of the others. How are we to account, then, for the behaviour and character of the majority of groups? For it is not something which can be regarded by the student as self-evident, self-explanatory, which can be simply taken for granted, or which can be dismissed as just "natural." The explanation, we suggest, can be traced to two main complementary and mutually dependent sources, or systems, which combine to produce the results we have had described to us. These two main factors are:

(1) the mechanisms and limitations of group expression underlying the behaviour of the group as a united whole;

(2) the mechanisms and limitations of individual expression underlying the behaviour of the majority of the individual members of the group.

While we have differentiated between these two systems, it should be clearly grasped that there is no sharp line of division between them; they tend, in other words, to shade into one another. One aspect of this is in the variable size of groups – the quantitative aspect. A single individual, for example, can be regarded, at the one extreme of size, as constituting the smallest possible group: i.e., a group containing one member. Here, as is obvious, the individual and the group coincide. Another aspect is the qualitative one: the variable qualitative level of groups – and this we will deal with later.

Now, if we consider for a moment the behaviour of the group as a whole, it will be clear that the ideas and feelings capable of group or mass expression, can only be of the simplest, most limited kind. While simple ideas such as those expressing agreement or disagreement, hatred or affection, contempt, anger or admiration, can be readily voiced by the crowd in the shouting of single words ("Yes!" "No!") and short slogans – or by cheering, booing, hissing, clapping, laughing, groaning, stamping, etc. – the more complicated ideas involving wordy explanation and complex processes of reasoning are, in virtue of this, incapable of mass expression. If the more complex ideas are expressed in the presence of a group then they can only be voiced by the individual, as such, who stands apart from the group and puts himself, in a certain sense, in opposition to it. This implies a measure of discipline and organisation, for such individual expression can only be accomplished if and when the group inhibits itself, or is suppressed, into silence and non-expression. In this connection we may recall the frequently observed and well-known fact that the vast majority of the members of a group are very reluctant to emerge, to put themselves apart from the group, and voice themselves as individuals. While they may like to do so, their fear of the group is so great that they would rather remain submerged and anonymous. But as members of the group, with their identity and individuality obliterated, they will shout, sing, clap, roar, laugh, hiss, and behave generally, quite without reserve, fear or apprehension. "Stage-fright" and "microphone-fright" are other examples of the same thing.

Conventionality, or conformity, in modes of public behaviour, dressing etc., are again familiar instances of this submersion of independent individuality for fear of opposing the group. "What will the neighbours think?" is a common phrase which will expresses the ingrained conservatism of the masses, the huge majority of people, who model their lives very largely on considerations of this sort. Fear of what other people will think, or say, or do, is nothing more than another instance of the individual's deep-rooted fear of putting himself in opposition to the group.

Here, then, when we contemplate the inherent limitations of group expression, on the one hand, and the universality of the individual's fear of the group, on the other, we may feel we are approaching the explanation of the phenomena of mass suggestion, "emotional contagion," of mass irrationality, intolerance, enthusiasm, impulsiveness, respect for force, and the whole host of characteristics which, as we have seen, are typical of the behaviour of large groups and crowds.

We shall, however, have to account for the intellectual, objective, reasoning, independently thinking minority of people who, according to Chakotin, tend to resist all suggestion; and, since they form a kind of group, to describe and explain their typical modes of behaviour, thinking and feeling, and how these modes differ qualitatively from those of the masses. Again, we shall have to account for the individual's dread, itself, of the group, and also its great ubiquity.

But before we pass on to discuss these important issues we shall draw attention to some interesting matters which closely relate to the results of our discussion so far.

We have reached the point where we perceive, more or less clearly, a striking feature in the psychological relationship of the individual to the group, namely: the dread or fear in which isolation or opposition to the group is universally regarded by the individual. We perceive, too, that this fear compels the individual to submerge his individuality and efface himself in the group, where he feels at his ease. It is this fear which makes him shrink from asserting his independence of the group, of putting himself apart from it, of performing any act, having any thoughts or intentions which could be regarded as contrary to the ideas and intentions of the group as a whole, or as isolating him from it as an individual. We see, also, that if group expression is limited by its inherent nature to the simplest and crudest of ideas and sentiments, then, because of this deep-seated fear, each individual taking part in group expression will be similarly limited.

The latent feelings of dread and guilt – which arise (sometimes accompanied by blushing or signs of embarrassment) in a person when his individuality threatens to emerge from self-effacement in the group, or when, inadvertently, the attention of the group becomes fixed on him are also intimately connected with the hostility, the disapproval and condemnation with which the group member regards any attempt on the part of another to preserve an independent or critical attitude; the unity and existence of the group are threatened and those who resist the mass suggestion, who do not conform, are therefore a menace and must be suppressed. For the same reason hostility is felt towards all other groups which threaten the disruption of one's own group. Within the group the individual feels strong; outside of it, on his own, he feels weak: "There's safety in numbers" says the old tag of popular wisdom with deep truth.

Thus, we see that dread of the group, on the part of each individual member, appears to constitute a common factor and an underlying basis for all or many of the typical attributes and outstanding features of group behaviour. This dread, in the form of "fear of public opinion," is well known and often referred to by writers. But what is not well known and not properly understood is its tremendous importance, is that this fear lies right down at the very roots of an overwhelming amount of human social activity, emotion and thought, and is involved in many different forms of group behaviour from that of mere crowds to that of dispersed masses; and that – since at all times individuals are also members of different kinds of groups, either congregated or dispersed, either organised or unorganised – this dread is involved in a great deal of "individual" behaviour.

We can see, here, that this universal fear of the group is not unconnected with the so-called human herd instinct, or instinct of gregariousness. We shall also see that it is intimately associated with processes of the human mind which have been investigated and described, on the one side, by Freud and the psychoanalysts, and on the other, by Pavlov and the reflexologists.

This brings us briefly to touch upon the question of leadership in so far as it is related to dread of the group. It has been said above, that members of a group, because of the dread, shrink from isolating themselves as individuals, would rather remain in self-effacement within the group and hesitate, even to draw attention in any way to themselves personally as this also tends to put them apart. How then are we to account for the phenomenon of leadership, which, in one form or another, is practically as universal as fear of the group, and which figures so prominently in nearly all descriptions of group behaviour? How is it possible, if the dread is so universal, for men, wherever there are groups, to come forward or push themselves forward, establish themselves as leaders, and isolate themselves from the group as individuals? How is it that, in spite of the dread, there are always some individuals who do draw attention to themselves and even seem to enjoy doing so? It appears that we have to deal with something more than just dread of the group.

As is so often the case with the human mind, it seems that, underlying the surface of actual events, what we are really dealing with is the interaction of conflicting and opposing tendencies. In this case the opposing tendencies would appear to be (a), the instinctive egoistically impulses, which drive the individual into struggle with his fellows and into the desire to subject them to himself, and (b), the fear of the group. To put it crudely but simply: the interaction is between the feeling or desire for personal, individual power, and fear of the power of the group. As we mentioned above the majority of the members of a group are reluctant to emerge and voice themselves as independent individuals *though they may desire to do so.*

Since the conflict between these opposing tendencies is going on, more or less unconsciously, all the time in the individual, then we can conclude that a large proportion, at least, of human behaviour – both group and individual behaviour – is in great measure due to it, and becomes more explicable in terms of this opposition. Much of Freud's work has gone to show that this is, indeed, the true position. According to him there is something like a state of perpetual warfare, going on within each individual, between the id, which "stands for the untamed passions," and the super-ego, "the representative of all the moral restrictions," which can be "traced back to the influence of parents, teachers and so on" (*New Introductory Lectures on Psychoanalysis*).

Briefly, then, we can say that the instinctive egoist impulses of the leader of a group and also of the person who emerges to voice himself as an individual – or who deliberately attracts attention to himself – have to a large extent overcome the fear of isolating themselves from their particular groups, have overcome the compulsion to remain anonymous. In general, however, as Freud himself says, "The fear of the super-ego should normally never cease, since it is indispensable in the social relations in the form of moral anxiety, and it is only in the rarest instances that an individual succeeds in becoming independent of the community." (*New Introductory Lectures on Psychoanalysis*, p.116.)

We are reminded, here, of Chakotin's references to the active 10 percent and the passive 90 percent and also of Hitler's distinction between the few, the leaders, and the passive, "sheep-like" masses.

There are, of course, other, more complex and deeper considerations involved in this complicated question of the individual in his relation to the group and to the leader. But we shall attempt to come to some understanding of these in later pages.

Before proceeding to discuss the smaller but more intellectual types of group it remains for us to observe how these mass modes of behaviour, thinking and feeling are discernible in large-scale political movements, particularly in those of Right-wing and fascist politics. In other words, what we wish to show is that the more exclusively Right-wing a political movement is, the more will its *political* action, feeling, and thinking, clearly exhibit these *mass* or *collectivist* modes of behaviour. We have already seen in an earlier chapter that the economic content of Right-wing modes of political behaviour is *economic individualism*; that is to say, an identification with *economic* individualism is the basic subject-matter, the fundamental content, of Right-wing political forms of expression. We have since learnt that these political forms or modes (characteristic of the Right-wing masses) are, in themselves, highly *collectivist* political modes.

Thus, in fastening our attention upon the *form* or mode of political expression, as distinct from its *content* or subject-matter – by examining the characteristics of the *modes* of political expression instead of discussing the attributes of their economic contents – we arrive at the concept of *political collectivism*. And, moreover, the concept of political collectivism can now be clearly distinguished from the concept of economic collectivism – which, as we saw in Chapter 2, is the basic economic content or subject-matter with which the Left-wing minority identify themselves.

It appears, then, that attachment to the idea of economic individualism necessarily involves attachment to a mode of expression which can now be described as political collectivism. We may possibly anticipate the further development that, at the other extreme of our political scale, attachment to the idea of *economic collectivism* also necessarily involves an attachment to a mode of expression which we can now describe as *political individualism*. We shall, in fact, find this to be the case.

1.6 Political Collectivism

PARADOXICALLY enough, it is to fascism that we have to turn in order to find the political movement and expression most exclusively representative of the real masses – to find, in other words, the mass movement *par excellence*, the supreme example of political collectivism. This curious paradox was well expressed by Goebbels when he declared that the Nazi regime was more democratic than democracy. It is also clearly reflected in this shrewd observation by Le Bon (who, though he had a contempt for democracy, had an insight into the psychology of masses) in which he predicts that the advent to power of the crowd or mass will bring with it "a barbarian phase": "Universal symptoms show in all nations the rapid growth of the power of the crowd. The advent of the crowd will, perhaps, mark one of the last of the Western civilisations, a return to the periods of confusion and anarchy which precede the emergence of new societies." How ironically true of fascism, the supreme spokesman of the crowd, the most accurate, the most exclusive interpreter of the ideology of the vast, apolitical, unobjective, emotional masses.

As is well known to those engaged in the practical donkey-work of political activity, the majority of people in democratic countries have very little real interest, even of the passive kind, in political issues – particularly the basic ones – and have still less *active* interest in the democratic political parties. Even at election times, which do not come often, serious discussion of real issues is rare and undertaken only by the minority – while, if a majority do actually vote, it is frequently not large and has to be stimulated, bribed, threatened or cajoled by electioneering stunts, scares, flattery, car rides, festivities, sensational accusations and counter-charges, and other equally non-political attractions. But, with all this clamour and publicity, it is usual for a substantial percentage of the electorate to remain indifferent and to ignore their democratic rights.

The contemplation and realisation of these facts may cause unpleasant emotions of disappointment and despair in those more thoughtful, democratic individuals who – presuming the coming of universal enlightenment – are hopefully and ever seeking for signs of it among the masses and in day-to-day political affairs. In order to spare themselves these unpleasant feelings there is a danger that they may tend to gloss lightly over the facts. But for science and scientific understanding the hard facts cannot be ignored or glossed over; they must be squarely faced. Our wishes, emotions and declarations of faith in human nature are irrelevant when we are seeking to establish factual, scientific truth. And the evidence abounds for those who seek it and have eyes to see.

Fascism, as we have said, is the most exclusive representative of the political collectivism of the masses. Many books by students of fascism include indirect references to this political collectivism when they refer to the "mass state," "mass enthusiasm," "collectivist state," "mass thinking," etc. Chamberlain, in his book *A False Utopia*, quotes an editor of Nazi Germany as saying: "We have become a nation of mass meetings, mass theatres, mass celebrations, and mass elections." Chamberlain comments: "In the collectivist state the individual is completely submerged in the mass. A trained psychologist could find in each of them a remarkable illustration of the powers of mass hypnotism."

Referring to the famous Saar elections of January, 1935 – when Saarlanders had the choice of remaining democratic (either by choosing to continue under the existing League of Nations' administration or by becoming part of France) or of going fascist and becoming part of Germany where the Nazis had been in power for two years – Konrad Heiden, in *One Man Against Europe* (1939) writes:

> Hitler was in power in Germany and his government aroused enthusiasm in many, but in many fear and hatred. The horrors of the concentration camps, the bloody deeds of the 30th June, 1934, were better known in Saar territory, when the press was free at least in name, than in Germany where every word was watched. The suppression of the workers' trades unions and the persecution of the Catholic Church was bound to arouse uneasiness in a population which consisted almost entirely of miners and metal workers and 60 percent of which were Catholics. (p. 159.)
>
> On the morning of the voting 50,000 National Socialists called on wavering voters and assured them that there were no secrets. Anyone who voted against his own country would be found out and called to account in a concentration camp. In fact the voting, supervised by a League commission took place with exemplary order. But most of the voters no longer believed in the secrecy of the ballot, any more than voters in Germany believe in it. Above all the nationalist watchword proved to be irresistible; it attracted voters who even shortly before had been doubtful. It was irresistible, too, because no conception of political reality adhered to the cause of the League; there was no vital force in it. The people of the Saar saw in practice only Germany on the one side and France on the other. So on the 13th January, 1935, 477,000 Saarlanders voted for Germany and only 46,000 for the League of Nations. That represented 9.3 percent against 8.8 percent. Only 2,000 voted for France. (p. 167.)

Of Hitler and the power of suggestion, Heiden says:

> In his good hours he exerts a power of suggestion which would be surprising if shown in an experimental demonstration, but we must always remember that a mighty suggestive power precedes the German dictator before his actual appearance... we must remember the extreme impressionability of crowds under sustained influence, and also how long the world has now been exposed to the suggestions of National Socialism.
>
> With the advantages of this suggestion, extraordinary propagandist risks can be taken. People can be made to believe things when the proof of the contrary is staring them in the face. Hitler has injected into a large number of people all over the world the idea that he is loyal to his convictions. In fact, he only clings to them – so long as they serve his purpose. He is the perfect representative of a political movement which has no real belief except in the practice of ruling, and no principle except to have an answer for every situation, and as such he changes his basic views as and when required.
>
> ... The German people is already being transformed into a

mechanical chorus, for it is no longer its mental attitude that counts, but only its technical approval. The symbol of this mechanisation is the extraordinary desk or lectern from which Hitler speaks. In an unguarded moment a man named Boese, on the authority of the head of the German Radio, gave the following particulars of it. 'This desk, of which at that time, the spring of 1936, there were five examples, has a number of buttons, by means of which Hiter gives certain signals while he is speaking; he gives the sign for film photographs to be taken and for the dimming or brightening and the direction of the searchlights. By thus regulating the mood of the audience he increases the will to applaud until at another signal the Storm Troops by clapping and shouting let loose general applause...'

Under the glare of searchlights, thus controlled by his suggestion-machine, human beings are lost to sight and nothing remains but the inchoate mass, the mechanical chorus... Crowds applaud, individuals may still contradict. One of his close acquaintances said in confidence, 'If he discovers among ten thousand shouters one man with a grim look on his face, Hitler's day is spoilt.' (pp. 275-6.)

Again and again we have evidence from the statements of fascists themselves that their worship of the state is no more than the worship of the primitive group. R. A. Brady, in *The Spirit and Structure of German Fascism*, quoting from *Deutsches Kulturrecht* Hamburg, 1936, says that the Nazis regard:

... the state as a natural community – a natural community made up of a people fused together through ties of blood, speech, customs, and common experiences, and which in its most fully developed form we characterise by the term nation. The nation is fixed and eternal, and stands at the centre of all historical and political experience.

The culture of this state comes out of a wholly simple, wholly primitive perception of the people, and in obedience to their will and law. Since it grows out of the people it cannot be commanded from above... it is not a state function, since it is no less than the spiritual side of the people's life and being. As actualisation of the feeling and will of the people, the principles which underlie it can in nowise be clarified and formulated. (pp. 84-5.)

Quoting again from the same source Brady goes on:

speaking of the difference between the pre-liberal and the Nazi cultural authoritarianism, they offer this contrast: Authority for National Socialism comes out of the people itself, not out of a power which rules superior over it; the will of the state comes out of the folkways, is free, sovereign, and of a new type. The will of the state is the will of the people, and this is not to be found on the surface of daily life and in day by day interests, but only where the final and partially unconscious longing is formed. That is to say, out of the national soul.

... How, then, is this authority determined? The answer is worth quoting in full:

Out of the national soul emerges the law from which the National Socialist leader derives his legitimation and his policies. He is not thus an organ of will superior to the people, but *instrument of the will of the people which exists in him.* Who rules the people of its own will, and who expresses the character of the National Socialist state in two syllables, we know as *The Leader.*

Leader is the opposite of magistrate. Who leads does not determine the objectives arbitrarily and by himself; that is done by the led. The led are the people. *But the Leader knows the goal and knows the direction . . . Who carries this spirit in him, who knows the direction is the Leader.* (pp. 85-6.)

In other words, he who best speaks with the voice of the masses, of the group, he who most accurately voices their thoughts and interprets their feelings, he is the popular leader. Apropos of this, it is interesting to note that Dr. C. G. Jung, the Swiss psychiatrist, who was "personally fascinated by the problem of Hitler's personality, and had studied it for years," has said (H. R. Knickerbocker's *Is Tomorrow Hitler's?* 45-6): "... Hitler is the mirror of every German's unconscious... He is the loud-speaker which magnifies the inaudible whispers of the German soul until they can be heard by the German's conscious ear. He is the first man to tell every German what he has been thinking and feeling all along in his unconscious... His Voice is nothing other than his own unconscious, into which the German people have projected their own selves; that is, the unconscious of seventy-eight million Germans. That is what makes him powerful." "Hitler," said Jung, "listens and obeys. The true leader is always led."

Heiden, in his *Der Fuehrer*, says much the same thing when he writes:

With unerring sureness Hitler expressed the speechless panic of the masses faced by an invisible enemy and gave the nameless spectre a name. He was a pure fragment of the modern mass soul, unclouded by any personal qualities. One scarcely need ask with what arts he conquered the masses; he did not conquer them, he portrayed and represented them. His speeches are day-dreams of this mass soul; they are chaotic, full of contradictions, if their words are taken literally, often senseless... often they can be refuted by reason, but they follow the far mightier logic of the subconscious, which no refutation can touch. Hitler has given speech to the speechless terror of the modern mass, and to the nameless fear he has given a name. That makes him the greatest mass orator of the mass age... (pp. 90-1.)

He does not dominate the minds of millions, his mind belongs to them. Like a piece of wood floating on the waves, he follows the shifting currents of public opinion. This is his true strength.

The true aim of political propaganda is not to influence, but to study, the masses... (p. 117.)

Further confirmation of the fact that fascism and fascist leaders represent the most exclusive expression of the mass or group modes of behaviour, thinking and feeling – represent, in a word, the supreme example of political collectivism – comes from Mussolini himself. In his book, *My Autobiography*, he declares:

I have made a profound study of the interests, the aspirations and the tendencies of our masses... I cover with my contempt dishonest and lying opponents, slanderers, deniers of the Country, and everyone who drowns every sense of dignity, every sentiment of National and human solidarity is the filthy cesspool of low grudges. Defeated ones who cluck to the wind, survivors of a building which toppled for ever, accomplices in the ruin and shame in which the Country was going to be dragged, sometimes do not even have the dignity of silence...

I am strict with my most faithful followers... I am near to the heart of the masses and listen to its beats, I read its aspiration and interests. I know the virtue of the race. I probe at its purity and soundness. (p. 251.)

It is noticeable what a great part is played by the individual's "fear of the group" under fascism. As we have inferred, this fear is omnipresent in every society, but under fascism it becomes greatly emphasised and ruthlessly exploited.

"The structure of the Third Reich cannot be understood," says Konrad Heiden, referring to the Nazi Gestapo, "without this monstrous apparatus for intimidation. In the beginning is fear, the state is all-powerful, obedience is the fount and source of all things. And yet it would, be a mistake if we thought of the German people's fear of its government as synonymous with aversion. No, there is enthusiasm. This contradiction between mob-enthusiasm and police rule is one of the mysteries of dictatorship, and seems almost to suggest that the object of enthusiasm is police-rule itself. Does the slave derive happiness from the presence of the jack-boot on his neck? It is certain that relief from responsibility has always been a substantial element in the happiness of the mob – the submersion of the man in the mass, no matter whether he be high or low, educated or uneducated." (*One Man Against Europe*, pp. 105-6.) Note especially the words "In the beginning is fear, the state is all-powerful, obedience is the fount and source of all things." In this fear of the all-powerful state – to which the individual must be completely subjected, subservient and obedient – we can easily recognise the clearest possible example of our concept of the individual's fear of the all-powerful group. The underlying, universal dread of the group is, indeed, one of the main keys to the understanding of fascism, of the "contradiction between mob enthusiasm and police rule," of the "mysteries of dictatorship."

The complete and utter political subordination of the individual to the omnipotent, omnipresent fascist state – the exclusive, totalitarian political organisation of the "national" or "racial" group, i.e., of the masses – is a favourite theme of fascist leaders and spokesmen. In his *No Compromise*, Melvin Rader, in a chapter headed "Race, State and Individual," writes:

Repeatedly in Fascist literature, the State is said to be an organism or group mind. Mussolini speaks of the State as having a will and as being itself conscious. Alfredo Rocco has declared that the State is an organism distinct from the citizens who at any time compose it, and has its own life and its ends higher than those of individuals, to which those of individuals must be subordinated. Similarly Walther Darré, Nazi Minister of Agriculture, has referred to the State as a super-organic organism, which exacts devotion, sacrifice of the individual, and abandonment of egoism for the sake of a higher aim. (p. 230.)

In discussing the ideas of Gentile, the Italian fascist, Rader continues:

> Gentile means by spirit, moreover, not the separate and individual mind, which he regards as an unreal abstraction, but the one universal Person to which we all belong: the *one man* in whom all individuals are united and with whom they are all identified. He accordingly exalts the collective mind at the expense of individual freedom: In the way of conclusion, then, it may be said that I, as a citizen, have indeed a will of my own; but that upon further investigation my will is found to coincide exactly with the will of the State, and I want anything only in so far as the state wants me to want it. (p. 250.)

Further on:

> ... the Fascists worship the parochial community. They have created a new collectivism, narrow, intolerant and repressive. Whether the object of worship be called the State or the Race, the totalitarian community is primarily the expression of collective selfishness, opposed to the super-national interests of Western culture, and equally opposed to the freedom of individual personalities. Fascism affords no rich and inclusive unity, but a monotonous uniformity. Only a servile mind could regard this servile society as the highest of values. (p.318.)

Additional evidence of fascism's conformity with group behaviour, in respect of its hostility to, and suppression of, the independent individual and independent thinking, is to be found in the following quotations give by Professor Gangulee:

> The Nation and not the Individual is the first concern of the Law. (Nazi Party Slogan.)
>
> Not only the individual, but all cultural organisations have therefore in the last resort to serve the community of the people, and it is in relation to this that they get their meaning and justification. To this extent only a political activity is to be recognised and tolerated in the life of the people. Therefore economics, law, science, art, religion have no independence; they have all to be political. Thus, even law is to be determined in a way that is at variance with the formal conception hitherto prevailing. What serves the state is right, what injures it is wrong. (Professor Wilhelm Sauser: *Philosophy of the Law and of the State*, 1936.)
>
> There is no freedom of the individual. There is only freedom of peoples, nations or races; for these are the only material and historical realities through which the life of the individual exists. (Dr. Otto Dietrich, addressing students of the University of Berlin, 1937.)
>
> In the National-Socialist conception of the state the problem of protecting the individual against the state does not arise. National Socialism defends the people as a whole against the individual, when and wherever his interests are not in harmony with the general welfare of the whole German people... Since the state consists of the totality of its citizens, united in a common destiny by common

blood and a common philosophy of life and comprised in a single Party organisation, it is neither necessary nor possible to define a sphere of freedom for the individual citizen as against the state... (From the *Beamtenkalender*, 1937.)

The National-Socialist Government has dissolved the Trade Unions and the Federations of employers. 'It will oppose anyone and anything tending to divide the people into groups. (Dr. Ley: *Germany Speaks*, 1938.)

The German journalist... will only be able to discharge this duty if he identifies himself with the creative idea of the state. (George Foerster: *Freedom in the Authoritarian State*, 1933.)

Hear nothing that we do not wish you to hear. See nothing that we do not wish you to see. Believe nothing that we do not wish you to believe. Think nothing that we do not wish you to think. (Goebbels.)

Freedom means to be bound by the ties of race... and this demands *protection* of the race. (Alfred Rosenberg.)

The slogan of objective science has been coined by the professoriate simply in order to escape from the very necessary supervision by the power of the state. What is called the crisis of science is nothing more than that the gentlemen are beginning to see of their own accord how they have gone off the line with their objectivity and independence. (Hitler to Rauschning.)

The old idea of science based on the sovereign right of abstract intellectual activity has gone forever... The true freedom of science is to be an organ of a nation's living strength and of its historic fate... (Dr. Rust, Nazi Minister of Education, at the centenary of Heidelberg University.)

The Party takes over the function of what has been society – that is what I wanted them to understand. The Party is all-embracing. It rules our lives in all their breadth and depth. We must therefore develop branches of the Party in which the whole of individual life will be reflected. Each activity and each need of the individual will thereby be regulated by the Party as the representative of the general good. There will be no license, no free space in which the individual belongs to himself... Of what importance is that if I range men firmly within a discipline they cannot escape? Let them then own land or factories as much as they please. The decisive factor is that the state, through the Party, is supreme over them, regardless whether they are owners or workers. (Hitler to Rauschning, 1934.)

Finally, in order to show that the complete subjection of the independent, thinking individual (i.e. the intellectual) to the "state," "nation," or "race" that is, to the organised group or masses – is quite typical of fascism, and moreover, is one of its keystones, We give a few samples from the spokesmen of Italian fascism.

Mussolini, for instance, in *The Political and Social Doctrine of Fascism* (Hogarth Press) asserts:

The principle that society exists solely through the well-being and the personal liberty of all the individuals of which it is composed does not appear to be conformable to the plans of nature, in whose workings the race alone seems to be taken into consideration, and the individual sacrificed to it... (quoting Renan, p. 16.)

But the Fascist negation of Socialism, Democracy and Liberalism must not be taken to mean that Fascism desires to lead the world back to the state of affairs before 1789, the date which seems to be indicated as the opening years of the succeeding semi-Liberal century... Absolute monarchy has been and can never return, any more than blind acceptance of ecclesiastical authority... (p. 19.)

For if the nineteenth century was a century of individualism (Liberalism always signifying individualism) it may be expected that this will be the century of collectivism, and hence the century of the State... the doctrines of Democracy are the heirs of the Encyclopedists... (p. 20.)

The foundation of Fascism is the conception of the State, its character, its duty, and its aim. Fascism conceives of the State as an absolute, in comparison with which all individuals or groups are relative, only to be conceived of in their relation to the State... (p. 21.)

The State is the guarantor of security both internal and external, but it is also the custodian and transmitter of the spirit of the people, as it has grown up through the centuries in language, in customs and in faith. And the State is not only a living reality of the present, it is also linked with the past and above all with the future, and thus transcending the brief limits of individual life, it represents the immanent spirit of the nation... (p. 22.)

... but whoever says Liberalism implies individualism, and whoever says Fascism implies the State...(p. 23.)

Fascism desires the State to be a strong and organic body, at the same time reposing upon broad and popular support... The Fascist State organises the nation, but leaves a sufficient margin of liberty to the individual; the latter is deprived of all useless and possibly harmful freedom, but retains what is essential; the deciding power in this question cannot be the individual, but the State alone. (p. 24.)

Melvin Rader gives the following:

For we know now that a natural, native, initial liberty does not exist between State and individual, but rather that they are united in a biological unity. Political liberty must take this fact into account, it must make it its norm. This is the *punctum saliens* of the new Italian political culture, this is the revolution of principles. In order to regulate the relationship between State and individual, they must no longer be looked upon as separate entities; they must be perceived in their biological unity. (Enrico Corradini: *La Riforma Politica in Europe*, p. 100.)

For Liberalism, the individual is the end and society the means; nor is it conceivable that the individual, considered in the dignity of an ultimate finality, be lowered to mere instrumentality. For

Fascism, society is the end, individuals' the means, and its whole life consists in using individuals as instruments for its social ends. . . Individual rights are only recognised in so far as they are implied in the rights of the State. (Alfredo Rocco: "The Political Doctrine of Fascism," *International Conciliation*, Oct. 1926, pp. 402-3.)

The liberty of the individual coincides perfectly with obedience to the State, that is to say, with the realisation of that ultimate good for which the individual himself lives and works and through which he becomes a participant in history and in the divine life. (Roberto Farinacci, "Render unto Caesar ," *Living Age*, Jan. 1939, p. 410.)

Rader comments:

Mussolini, in a like manner, affirms that the individual exists only in so far as he is within the State and subjected to the requirements of the State, and that the individual in the Fascist State is not annulled but rather multiplied. The Nazis also insist that the individual can achieve freedom and personal dignity only by identifying himself with the race, the nation and the State. Personality, declares Rosenberg, does not stand in an alien relationship to the masses, but is the highest expression of the national will.

The reader will have noticed, in the above quotations, that fascism's antipathy to individual independence of mind – in other words, to intellectualism – is there clearly identified with its uncompromising opposition to the Left-wing, i.e. to "Socialism, Democracy and Liberalism."

We have said that the mass modes of thought and behaviour – based largely on a strong dread (latent or otherwise) of opposing the group – which are characteristic of groups of the larger or more primitive type, are also more characteristic of the political creeds of the Right than of the Left. And, we have previously noted, the parties of the Right tend, on the whole, to be the mass parties, or rather, to be those parties with greater support in the community, to be parties with mass followings. We have just seen, from an examination of fascist ideology (the extreme Right-wing) and its typical utterances, how well the relevant political and ideological facts support our theory. Let us now look cursorily at conservatism, the second Right-wing outlook, and see how well our ideas fit the facts of the conservative ideology.

Considered in relation to our original scale of political opinion, conservatism presents us with a distinct qualitative transition from the fascist outlook. For instance, fascism is inherently and unalterably anti-democratic; its hostility towards all other outlooks is absolute and uncompromising. Conservatism, on the other hand, tends to be moderately democratic and compromising in its attitude towards all other political groupings. The fascist ideology, as we have seen, utterly and emphatically rejects logic, theory, discussion, arbitration etc., and particularly individual independence of thought. Though conservatism may not fervently and fanatically extol these things it nevertheless definitely rejects the complete, absolute intolerance of them characteristic of the fascist attitude. This "rejection of rejection" marks the first major qualitative change or transition, the first major negation of negation, in the development of ideology and in the vertical growth of intellect.

Nevertheless, by a comparative examination of the ideological material – that is, of the fascist and conservative modes of behaviour, thought, feeling – we can easily detect such similarity in the characteristic features of the conservative outlook to some of the features typical of fascism, even though, in the process of development they may have undergone important modifications.

The conservative's strong identification with the national group, the nation, the race (national unity, "bull dog breed" etc.); his love of heroes and of strong, forceful leadership, of "character" rather than of intellect or understanding; his preference for practical action over theoretical consideration; his admiration for discipline, personal power, patriotism, courage, bravery, militaristic and physical qualities generally; his pride in "Empire," national honour and national, racial superiority (Britain rules the waves); his assumption of the *inborn* inferiority of the masses and the necessity for a biologically determined (by superior birth and breeding) elite or ruling caste; his tendency to rely on "instinct" and feeling for political guidance, and to distrust reason or logic; his liking for symbols and symbolism, especially those relating to the national or racial group (Britannia, Royalty, the national flag and colours, patron saints, John Bull, "St. George for Merrie England" etc.); his aversion for social, economic or racial "equality," for "internationalism" and Left-wing ideas generally; his sympathy and reverence for authority, hierarchy, mysticism and the "glorious" racial past – all these features of the typical conservative outlook are plainly seen to be closely related to the characteristic mass modes of the behaviour and thought of primitive groups in general, and of fascism in particular.

It is a significant fact that fascists reserve most of their political intolerance for the violent vilification of liberalism, socialism and communism, and have little to say about conservatism as such.

The study of mass modes of behaviour and their underlying mechanisms helps to shed light on many problems and everyday events concerning the bigger political groups, particularly those of the Right-wing.

It is interesting, for instance, to observe that a well-known and oft-remarked fact – namely, that open schisms, splits and factious disputes occur less frequently among members of the Right-wing than among those of the Left – becomes more intelligible in the light of "the individual's identification with, and fear of, the group" (which prevails more strongly among the members of the larger type of group, and consequently becomes a strong, unifying force in Right-wing politics). The conservative tendency of most people to "go with the crowd, with the majority" will readily come to mind in this connection and is too well-known to require any emphasis. "Rebellious Tories," it is often remarked by their critics, "are soon brought to heel by the crack of the whip." "The Left," frequently remark the conservatives, "are always squabbling among themselves."

Thus we can see that our concepts of "political collectivism," "dread of the group," "vertical development of intellect" etc., apply equally well to both the conservative and the fascist modes of expression, and to the qualitative relations and distinctions between them. It should be stressed and made quite clear, however, that, despite the many similarities in their ideologies and the fact that they occupy vertically adjacent positions in the political scale, conservatism, from this very point of view, does represent a major and real qualitative modification of the fascist attitude; and that politically and ideologically, a wider gulf separates them than is frequently supposed among some of their critics of the extreme Left, who tend merely to lump them together.

The fact is that democratic conservatism, as with any other democratic political outlook, represents an ideological level which – because of its modification of the common, primitive assumptions – does not correspond with that occupied by a large and numerous section of the population. While the conservative ideology may express the general, negative political attitude of these people more nearly than the ideologies of the rest of democratic parties, this numerous section remains, on the whole, either weakly interested in politics or completely apathetic and indifferent. Only when fascism comes along, to express their real thoughts and feelings in an unmodified, unqualified, unconditioned form, does their indifference gradually depart and their "political" enthusiasm grow. Hence, one of the most important reasons for fascism's comparatively rapid growth and rise to political power: it represented the intolerant, uncompromising, largely negative ideology of the masses more clearly and surely than could either democratic conservatism or any of the other democratic groups.

1.7 Political Individualism

IN contrast to the larger type of political group – which, as we have seen from our brief study, tends on the one hand to adhere to "economic individualism" and, on the other, to "political collectivism" – we now come to consider the smaller type of group: that is to say, to consider those groups which have as their basic content or subject-matter (their intellectual or ideological material) the idea of "economic collectivism," and at the same time, "political individualism" as their basic mode or form of ideological expression.

It will be simpler and more convenient for the purposes of exposition to deal with groups drawn from the extreme Left. While our observations will be largely confined to these extremer minority groups and will apply preeminently to them, nevertheless, they will also apply, in lesser degree, to the less extreme Left. We might generalise and say: our observations will apply to other political groups with modifications proportional to their remoteness from the Left-wing extremity; and these modifications will increasingly partake of the nature of the mass modes of behaviour, thought and feeling we have already described, as we pass down the political scale to the extreme Right.

We have referred, in Chapter 3, to intellectualism as a general distinguishing characteristic of the Left-wing. We saw that the extreme Left especially was more concerned and identified with the typical features of intellectualism: abstract theory and principles, doctrine, objectivity, logic, reason, academic discussion and exposition etc. Hand in hand with these goes the repression of "subjective," "emotional" thinking, i.e., the rejection of emotional group suggestion and of emotional suggestibility – which, we have come to understand, is characteristic of mass behaviour and thinking, and largely based on the individual member's fear of being separated from the group, the so-called herd instinct. We have learnt, for example, in Chapter 4, from Chakotin, that the intellectual minority resist emotional suggestion but that they are not immune to rational, persuasive, objective argument.

The question naturally arises as to how this intellectual minority (intellectual in the vertical sense) comes to exist as such, how intellectuals come to separate themselves from the mass modes of expression. We shall attempt to account for this – together with the origin of dread of the group – more fully in Part II of this book. But it will be convenient to say something about it at this stage before we go on to treat of political individualism in intellectual groups. And for the time being it must suffice.

We have already shown (Chapter 5) that the group places severe restraints on the egoistic impulses of the individual; it imposes limitations, in other words, upon his means of self-assertion or self-expression. This view is here entirely in harmony with the psychoanalytic standpoint when Freud writes (in his *Introductory Lectures on Psychoanalysis*, p. 17): "We believe that civilisation has been built up, under the pressure of the struggle for existence, by sacrifices in gratification of the primitive impulses, and that it is to a great extent for ever being recreated, as each individual, successively joining the community, repeats the sacrifice of his instinctive pleasures for the common good."

Now, we have mentioned (in the same chapter) one way in which the conflict (between the egoistic impulses and the group restraints) results in victory for the individual over the group, one simple method by which the group member overcomes the severe limitations imposed upon him by group expression. That method is by becoming a leader of the group; i.e., by *yielding* to the mass modes of expression – as for example we have seen Hitler yielded to them, and as man in general, in order to manipulate gross matter, has to yield to the limitations matter imposes upon him. By *accepting* these mass modes, by *identifying* himself more closely, wholly, with them, the individual – by operating within their limiting framework can give vent to his egoistic impulses in organising, leading the group and becoming its spokesman. "Nature is never conquered unless obeyed." Hitler, we saw, conquered the masses only because he obeyed them.

But there is also another method by means of which the individual can overcome or avoid the group restraints: that is by withdrawal, by renunciation, by rejection of the mass modes of expression and retiring, withdrawing, from the mass group. This is the method which is pursued by the intellectual and it is, in fact, the mark of the qualitative or vertical intellectual advance. It means that the individual is no longer held to the ideological modes of the mass by the dread of separation from the group, or what amounts to the same thing, by the emotional tie of identification. It means that the individual's egoistic impulses are free to express themselves in the assertion of his independence of the group[1]. It means that he is freed from identification with the primitive assumptions of the mass ideology which previously compelled him to reject or ignore any ideas and feelings incompatible with those assumptions. A shackle is removed which hitherto mentally bound him. His mind is free to pursue and identify itself with – to bind him to – another, more advanced, set of ideas and assumptions.

There are two or three points in connection with this mental emancipation of the individual from bondage to the group, which should be stressed here.

Firstly, we should bear in mind that only the comparative few are able to withdraw from and renounce the group. We must remember the enormous moral pressure which is put upon the individual by the group, in the form of mass emotional suggestion, in order to ensure his conformity and adherence to the group modes of thinking. This mass suggestion – which Freud has shown (see his *Group Psychology and the Analysis of the Ego*) to be closely allied to hypnotism and hypnotic suggestion – ensures the conformity of the vast majority of the group members, and the suggestion often varies in its intensity simply in order to accomplish just that result. If, for instance, within a mass group there arises a comparatively strong, critical faction (composed of a number of individuals whose ties with the group have weakened) which threatens the group with dissension and disruption, the mass suggestion will increase in strength, volume, intensity and violence, until the former condition of mass conformity is again restored. One of the best examples of this process in action on a major scale was, indeed, the rise of fascism itself – consequent upon the growth, on the continent, of a strong, though still comparatively small, Left-wing movement. Further examples of the

---

[1] This independence of the mass group is not only expressed intellectually but in many other ways – e.g., circumstances permitting, in particular forms of behavior and aesthetic tastes, certain modes of dress, long hair, beards, etc.

same process, but on a smaller scale, are to be seen time and time again in everyday politics, particularly during election periods. This process is largely unconscious; it is almost automatic and can be crudely compared with the automatic action involved in the process of thermostatic control: when the temperature goes down the energy for maintaining it is automatically turned on until the former condition is restored and the supply of energy is diminished. So that, on the whole, only a few individuals can ever succeed in resisting the mass suggestion and thus succeed in freeing themselves from the ties of the mass group.

Secondly, it must be borne in mind that the alternative path of renunciation, as a means of overcoming or avoiding the limitations of thought and expression imposed by membership of the mass group, is not *deliberately* and *consciously* chosen by the individual, who is, in fact, largely unconscious of what is actually going on in his relations with the group.

Thirdly, the whole path of renunciation itself is long and complicated, and is accompanied or marked by a more or less well-defined series of intermediate stages, which lead upwards, as it were, through a series of levels, from groups of the mass type – exhibiting low vertical growth of intellect – to smaller groups of the intellectual type, with a high vertical development of intellect, and through these to the smallest type of group of them all: the type with only one member, the independent individual himself. This latter type tends to remain more or less of an ideal, for exceedingly few people indeed ever actually reach it or even approximate it. It will readily be seen that this brief description of the ascent of the developing intellectual through these various ideological levels, accords well with the facts of the existing structure of the whole system of political groups as shown in our original diagrammatic scale of political levels (Fig. 1).

Lastly, it must be understood that by renunciation, by withdrawing from the group, the individual only escapes the group's influence and constraints in a direct ideological sense. Though the intellectual may no longer identify himself with the mass group, though he may no longer feel bound to it, nevertheless it still remains to influence and limit him indirectly – for instance, in its stimulation of his opposition to it and in its tendency to drive him continually towards its antithesis: complete intellectual independence[1]. Moreover, it remains also to frustrate his newly acquired aims which, for their practical fulfillment, require the permanent conversion of the masses to his way of thinking – that is to say, require the collective modes of thought and behaviour (political collectivism, mass suggestion) together with their economic contents (economic individualism) to give way, *in the mass group itself*, permanently and enduringly, to *independent* modes of thought. In short, the very content (i.e. economic collectivism) of the intellectual's mode of thought (political individualism) presupposes the inevitable and eventual universality of his way of thinking and the complete decay or abolition of its antithesis: namely, economic individualism and political collectivism.

We shall see, in Part II of this study, how this underlying presupposition or assumption actually arises as the consequence, mainly, of an interaction between

---

[1]It is of interest to observe that the *Concise Oxford Dictionary* defines the word "intelligentsia" – which comes through the Russian (intelligentsiya) and Italian (intelligenza) from the Latin of intelligence "The part of a nation (especially the Russian) that aspires to independent thinking."

(a) the intellectual's repression of his internal tendencies or impulses to "subjective" or "emotional" thinking (mentioned above) to give way, in other words, to mass suggestion, and (b) his repression of the external limitations, the frustration of his aims, imposed upon him by the continued and omnipresent existence of the mass group.

Strictly speaking, of course, nobody is able to separate himself truly from the mass group and escape entirely its limitations and constraints. To do that would entail complete physical withdrawal from human society itself. The separation, which is only partial and incomplete, is merely that effected by the renunciation, or internal inhibition, of the group ties and mass ideological modes and assumptions. The individual, no matter with what other group he may identify himself, and though he may no longer directly identify himself with the mass modes of thought, still remains *nolens volens* part of the mass group and still – though in a different manner – under its influence. Again, the renunciation, repression or inhibition of the mass ideological modes (shown by the individual's resistance to mass suggestion) is never continuously permanent or even complete. The renunciation or repression, to put it another way, varies in its extent and in its intensity according to the continually changing external situation or environment of the individual. And the extent and intensity of the repression will vary also from person to person, according, that is, to the individual's psychobiological make-up in other directions. The intellectual himself thus still remains subject to group suggestion in many ways, particularly so where the contents or subject-matter of the suggestion appear to him to have no obvious relation to the basic assumptions or economic content of the mass ideology – in most of the multitudinous petty affairs of everyday life, for instance, and when he is enjoying a joke or being entertained. It is when the contents of the suggestion are such as to recall, by association, the basic assumptions or economic content of the mass ideology that the repression, which has perhaps been temporarily relaxed or in abeyance, is suddenly strengthened and his resistance is brought to bear against the suggestion.

The repression then manifests itself in the intellectual's verbal opposition and feeling of hostility to the economic content (economic individualism) of the mass ideology, in his rejection of the underlying assumptions, the modes of thinking and feeling characteristic of that ideology (such as, e.g., its identification with authority, strong leadership, action, personal power, heroes, hierarchy, character, physical bravery, aggressiveness, force, symbolism, mysticism etc. and its intolerance or rejection of intellect, logic, understanding, doctrine, reason, theory, academic discussion, objectivity etc.).

In so far as the intellectual's opposition, resistance, and his rejection of the mass ideology, is itself – because of the repression – partly emotional and irrational, then we can expect that he is still to some extent subject to emotional suggestion in respect of behaviour, ideas – and feelings which tend to support his own modes of thinking and their contents. We shall find this to be the case. Such suggestion, of course – though he does not recognise it as such – assists in the maintenance of the repression and, consequently, in preserving his mental comfort. On the other hand, ideas which appear to be – whether they are or not connected with, or to favour, the mass ideology, or ideas which threaten to disturb the renounced, repressed material – will frequently call forth a vigorous, irrational and emotional opposition. The resistance hardens, the repression is intensified, and he will either oppose at all costs, despite any irrationality he may show, in order to defend himself against the mental pain involved in the acceptance and return of repressed material, or he may – especially if what he opposes be more rational and scientific – remove himself bodily from the scene of his discomfort.

These words of Freud, though they were meant to describe another but not altogether dissimilar set of circumstances, are peculiarly apt here:

> Thus we could definitely ascertain that the same man would take up and then abandon his critical objections over and over again in the course of the analysis. Whenever we are on the point of bringing to his consciousness some piece of unconscious material which is particularly painful to him, then he is critical in the extreme; even though he may have previously understood and accepted a great deal, yet now all these gains seem to be obliterated; in his struggles to oppose at all costs he can behave just as though he were mentally deficient, a form of 'emotional stupidity.' If he can be successfully helped to overcome this new resistance he regains his insight and comprehension. His critical faculty is not functioning independently, and therefore is not to be respected as if it were; it is merely a maid-of-all-work for his affective attitudes and is directed by his resistance. When he dislikes anything he can defend himself against it most ingeniously; but when anything suits, his book he can be credulous enough. We are perhaps all much the same; a person being analysed shows this dependence of the intellect upon the affective life so clearly because in the analysis he is so hard-pressed... As we already know from Breuer's observations, it follows from the existence of a symptom that some mental process has not been carried through to an end in a normal manner so that it could become conscious; the symptom is a substitute for that which has not come through. Now we know where to place the forces which we suspect to be at work. A vehement effort must have been exercised to prevent the mental process in question from penetrating into consciousness and as a result it has remained unconscious; being unconscious it had the power to construct a symptom. The same vehement effort is again at work during the analytic treatment, opposing the attempt to bring the unconscious into consciousness. This we perceive in the form of resistances. The pathogenic process which is demonstrated by the resistances we call REPRESSION.
> (*Introductory Lectures on Psychoanalysis*, pp. 247-8.)

We must not imagine that the two processes we have described – that of renunciation and that of "mastering" the group – are simply mutually exclusive. The intellectual finds an outlet for his egoistic impulses in argumentation, discussion and debate – in which, because of his superior intellect, he is easily able to "master" and "defeat" representatives of the masses, exponents of the mass ideology. On the other hand, the leader – who actively masters the group by more closely identifying himself with and expressing its ideology – in a certain sense also renounces the group, that is to say, the *passive* mass; he withdraws from it – because of his *active* leadership – and comes to have a certain contempt for its passivity, its "sheep-like half-heartedness," as did Hitler and Mussolini for example.

64

Now, we have asserted that the characteristic mental outlook, attitude, or mode of thought of the intellectual – his typical basic form of political or ideological expression – is that of "political individualism" (or as we shall see, what amounts to the same thing, "ideological individualism") which we have opposed to the political or ideological collectivism of the masses. We have also stated that the economic content of the intellectual's mode of thought is that of economic collectivism, i.e., the common ownership and control of the social means of producing material wealth. Much evidence of this linking of political individualism and economic collectivism is to be found in the many political statements on record made by various Left-wing scientists, intellectuals and members of the intelligentsia generally, especially those of the extreme Left. These statements are to the effect that there ought to be, or there must be, or there is actually taking place, a widespread change in the *existing* social and political attitude of the masses; a change from mere blind, irrational belief and prejudice to a more critical independent mode of thought.

Consider, for instance, the following extracts from a pamphlet issued by a small political group of Left-wing intellectuals (which, although it has existed as a political party, aiming at mass support, since 1904, is very little known outside extreme Left-wing circles):

> ... Applicants for membership are required to sign the Declaration of Principles printed on the inside cover of this pamphlet, and are expected to satisfy the branch before which their application comes that they understand and accept the principles in question... A pamphlet of this kind is bound to make somewhat difficult reading for those who are not yet accustomed to a closely reasoned explanation of political and economic problems. Any reader who finds this to be his experience is urged not to be discouraged. The effort to understand the various clauses of our Declaration of Principles and to explore the lines of thought opened up in this pamphlet cannot fail to be of value, even if at first it presents a little difficulty...
>
> Let him take them up as a challenge to his intellect, and either convince himself of their truth or prove their falsity. Let him then bring his actions into line with his convictions, rejecting the socialist principles if he thinks them unsound, but adopting them and cleaving to them if he finds them true and unassailable.
>
> True, these principles and the policy they dictate offer nothing but battle and victory – nothing but the last arduous campaign of the class struggle and the fruits thereof. But it is sufficient. It must not be exchanged for the power and pelf of office and a place near the fleshpots of Egypt for a few who dub themselves leaders of the working-class.
>
> We who know the class to which we belong, and build up all our hopes on the capacity of its intellect, know that it will not be so exchanged. We know that the working-class, as a class, is capable of judging all things for itself, and of marching on to its emancipation under the guidance of its own avowed principles without leaders or use for leaders...

Note the emphasis on principles, understanding, intellect, "closely reasoned explanation," and particularly the rejection of the idea of leadership, which, as we have seen, is one of the fundamental ideas or assumptions of the mass ideology. This rejection is closely related to the anarchist's emphatic repudiation of leadership, authority, nationalism, militarism, the state, compulsion, personal power, physical force, money, etc., etc. – which becomes extremely interesting, for it can be plainly observed that these rejections are renunciations of just the very characteristic and typical features of the politico-ideological collectivism of the mass groups. Furthermore, we have learnt to suspect that the emphatic emotional repudiation is largely based on the intellectual's actual repression of these assumptions and attitudes – that is to say, that the emphatic rejection arises from the actual existence of the repressed, internally inhibited material.

The anarchist, we should well note, is pre-eminently the advocate of political individualism, of critical, individual independence of thought and personality. He is, ideally at least, a self-sufficient, one-man political group – able, by using his reason, to make all political decisions for himself, and, under anarchism, to enter voluntarily into the co-operative labour of anarchist society, in which all shall have equally free access to the commonly owned means of production and to the wealth produced. Thus we see that in the anarchist ideology, political individualism on the one hand and economic collectivism on the other are developed to the extreme, to the ultimate. (In passing, it is of interest in this connection to note that anarchism is usually considered by anarchists and, often by other members of the extreme Left in their conception of the "withering away of the state," to be the final and ultimate form of human society.)

As evidence of this extreme development embodied in the anarchist ideology, let us consider some typical statements from anarchist sources. The following come from Rudolf Rocker's *Anarcho-Syndicalism*:

> Anarchism is a definite intellectual current in the life of our time, whose adherents advocate the abolition of economic monopolies and of all political and social coercive institutions within society. In place of the present capitalistic economic order Anarchists would have a free association of all productive forces based upon co-operative labour, which would have as its sole purpose the satisfying of the necessary requirements of every member of society, and would no longer have in view the special interest of privileged minorities within the social union. In place of the present state-organisations with their lifeless machinery of political and bureaucratic institutions Anarchists desire a federation of free communities which shall be bound to one another by their common economic and social interests and shall arrange their affairs by mutual agreement and free contract. Anyone who studies at all profoundly the economic and political development of the present social system will easily recognise that these objectives do not spring from the Utopian ideas of a few imaginative innovators, but that they are the logical outcome of a thorough examination of the present day social maladjustments, which with every new phase of the existing social conditions manifest themselves more plainly and more unwholesomely. (pp. 9-10.)

> Power operates only destructively, bent always on forcing every manifestation of life into the straitjacket of its laws. Its intellectual form of expression is dead dogma, its physical form brute force. And

66

this unintelligence of its objectives sets its stamp on its supporters also and renders them stupid and brutal, even when they were originally endowed with the best of talents...

It was from the understanding of this that modern Anarchism was born and now draws its moral force. Only freedom can inspire men to great things and bring about intellectual and social transformations. The art of ruling men has never been the art of educating men and inspiring them to a new shaping of their lives. Dreary compulsion has at its command only lifeless drill, which smothers any vital initiative at its birth and can bring forth only subjects, not free men. Freedom is the very essence of life, the impelling force in all intellectual and social development, the creator of every new outlook for the future of mankind. The liberation of man from economic exploitation and from intellectual and political oppression, which finds its finest expression in the world-philosophy of Anarchism, is the first prerequisite for the evolution of a higher social culture and a new humanity. (p. 33.)

Next, we have the following extracts from Herbert Read's *The Philosophy of Anarchism*:

... Progress is measured by the degree of differentiation within a society. If the individual is a unit in a corporate mass, his life is not merely brutish and short, but dull and mechanical. If the individual is a unit on his own, with space and potentiality for separate action, then he may be more subject to accident or chance, but at least he can expand and express himself. He can develop – develop in the only real meaning of the word develop in consciousness of strength, vitality and Joy. All this may seem very elementary, but it is a fundamental distinction which still divides people into two camps. You might think that it would be the natural desire of every man to develop as all independent personality, but this does not seem to be true. Because they are either economically or psychologically predisposed, there are many people who find safety in numbers, happiness in anonymity, and dignity in routine. They ask for nothing better than to be sheep under a shepherd, soldiers under a captain, slaves under a tyrant. The few that must expand become the shepherds, the captains and leaders of these willing followers.

Such servile people exist by the million, but again I ask: What is our measure of progress? And again I answer that it is only in the degree that the slave is emancipated and the personality differentiated that we can speak of progress... (pp. 8-9.)

... The worth of a civilisation or a culture is not valued in the terms of its material wealth or military power, but by the quality and achievements of its representative individuals – its philosophers, its poets and its artists. We might therefore express our definition of progress in a slightly more precise form. Progress, we might say, is the gradual establishment of a qualitative differentiation of the individuals within a society. In the long history of mankind the

group is to be regarded as an expedient – an evolutionary aid...
But the further step, by means of which a civilisation is given its
quality or culture, is only attained by a process of cellular division,
in the course of which the individual is differentiated, made distinct
from and independent of the parent group. The farther a society
progresses, the more dearly the individual becomes the antithesis of
the group. (p. 10.)

... Creeds and castes, and all forms of intellectual and emotional
grouping, belong to the past. The future unit is the individual, a
world in himself, self-contained and self-creative, freely-giving and
freely receiving, but essentially a free spirit. (p. 12.)

Lastly, here are some quotations taken from a review of Arthur Koestler's *The Yogi
and the Commissar* in the anarchist paper *War Commentary* (19/?/45):

... At the other end of the scale we get the people who realise fully
that no good can arise from an authoritarian system of government,
who accept all the negative criticism of anarchism, yet who have in-
sufficient faith in man to see any alternative to authority... Koestler,
who is one of the most talented of the independent Left intellectuals
of this country... realises. All the faults in authoritarian societies up
to the present, he has sufficient concern for mankind to make him
continue in spite of this fact to hope for a social system that will
not partake of these faults, yet he has not made that ultimate act of
faith in the potentialities of man which results in the final rejection
of authority as the pattern of social relations and the acceptance of a
libertarian cooperation as the basis of the administration of society.
Koestler, like most of the Left intellectuals who have preserved their
independence of thought, is fully aware of the equivocal nature of
the position in which he finds himself, and his latest book, *The Yogi
and the Commissar*, is an attempt to investigate thoroughly the
position of the revolutionary intellectual and to prescribe some line
of development which might lead to more constructive results.

Koestler sees the dilemma of the intellectuals expressed in the
extremes of the Yogi and the Commissar...

Koestler himself, it can be seen, hovers uneasily between, seeing
the good in each of them, yet unable to reconcile these apparently
contradictory tendencies. The duality from which he suffers is shared
by many of his generation, and has resulted in that unfortunate
lack of direction which has led so many of our intellectuals into
compromised positions, into defending the lesser evil. Koestler puts
their position when he says: "The collapse of the revolutionary
movement has put the intelligentsia into a defensive position; the
alternative for the next few years is no more 'capitalism or revolution'
but to save some of the values of democracy and humanism or to
lose them all; and to prevent this happening one has to cling more
than ever to the ragged banner of 'independent thinking.'"

It becomes clearly evident from an examination of these representative samples
of the extreme Left-wing and anarchist outlooks – exhibiting as they do the

highest development of political individualism and economic collectivism – that there is contained within them, standing out with varying degrees of sharpness, the important implication which we have mentioned earlier in this chapter. The implication is, namely, that at some future date, near or remote, the mass modes of behaviour, thought and feeling will die out, will cease to exist as such; and that the masses themselves will, in freeing themselves from the group ties and the crude modes of group expression, permanently and universally adopt the critical, objective, independent mode of thought typical of the intellectual, together with its necessary corollary and content of "economic collectivism."

This implication is of supreme importance in our study, for it presupposes a certain form of intellectual, ideological and political evolution on the part of human society, which, if it corresponds with the facts, renders the implication valid and with it the general position of these outlooks. But if, on the other hand, that mode of development does not so correspond with fact – that is, with the actual mode of development – if, in short, the objective evidence is against it, then of course the implication is unsound and with it a great part of the outlook of which it is so fundamental a constituent. We might possibly have supposed and taken it for granted that, as it was of such vital importance, this aspect of the (qualitative) intellectual or ideological development of society, would have been investigated and dealt with by those – the rational and scientifically-minded intellectuals – the validity of whose politico-ideological position depends so much upon it. But such is not the case. We may look in vain through the literature of the whole of the Left-wing to find any clear recognition of the problem, let alone any attempt to investigate it. What we do find is a tremendous amount of matter devoted to the study of the *economic* aspects of history, science, philosophy, primitive society and institutions, social development and the structure of modern society etc. In this massive literature all intellectual, ideological and political development is usually treated as a kind of epiphenomenon or byproduct of the economic evolution of society. Nowhere do we find a conception of a real, independent ideological evolution – with its own laws, underlying processes and mechanisms peculiar to itself. And nowhere do we find any direct or positive evidence to support the implication to which we have referred; it is simply ignored.

These considerations alone would tend to force us logically to the conclusion that the implication is very largely an assumption – an assumption which is more or less unconsciously drawn upon in order to support a position otherwise sustained by a great deal of study and insight into the economic aspects of social phenomena and social development. The conclusion is further strengthened by the consideration of such references as those found in the above samples – and to be found liberally distributed throughout all such literature – references to "faith in the potentialities of man," to the building of "all our hopes" on mass rationality, etc., etc. Further, when we come to examine the objective evidence, the *actual* mode of ideological development itself, we find that so far from giving factual support for the assumption, it undermines and belies it; the evidence, as we shall see, points the other way, and, at the same time, provides us with a complete and satisfactory explanation of how the assumption itself arises, and of the necessity for the assumption to be made by those who make it.

At this point it will be convenient to refer once again to our broad scale of political opinion, and to integrate with it the main results, so far, of our discussion:

namely, the new concepts of *political (or ideological) collectivism and individualism.* We are thus enabled, by adding these terms in their appropriate places on the scale, to perceive readily and in a diagrammatic manner, the inverse-ratio relationship – of *economic* individualism and collectivism on the one hand, and *political* individualism and collectivism on the other – as it occurs in both the ideological structure of modern society and in the typical ideological or vertical development of intellect itself. See Fig. 2 below.

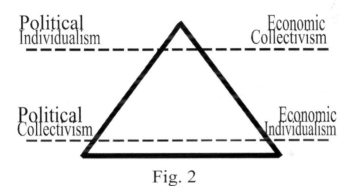

Fig. 2

1.8 The "Mass Rationality" Assumption

W<small>E</small> have now reached the position (a), wherein we recognise that the qualitative-intellectual or ideological development of the individual from mental dependence on the group (politico-ideological collectivism) towards complete mental independence (politico-ideological individualism) necessarily – through the development of its economic content – involves the adoption of what we shall call "the mass-rationality assumption," and (b), where we have already begun to suspect the validity of this assumption and to suspect that it arises, not on the basis of a rational study of the objective evidence of ideological evolution, but through some inner psychological need or process connected with the vertical development of intellect.Let us now relate these tentative results to what we have affirmed at the beginning of the previous chapter. We said that our conclusions would apply "in lesser degree, to the less extreme Left," that "our observations will apply to other political groups with modifications proportional to their remoteness from the Left-wing extremity" and that "these modifications will increasingly partake of the nature of the mass modes of behaviour, thought and feeling we have already described, as we pass down the political scale to the extreme Right."

Now that we know what to look for we can search through the literature of a wide variety of ideological types for examples of the mass-rationality assumption, and make an interesting comparative study of the result. It is most instructive. Limits of space prevent us from going into great detail, but we can at least give some general idea of the more important aspects of such a study, together with a few representative examples containing the assumption.

In the first place, we can confirm that, wherever we find the assumption, nowhere do we find that it is based on an objective study either of the intellectual-ideological development of the individual, or that of society. On the other hand, we find it most frequently based on the evidence and study of the *economic and scientific-technological* development of human society. (It is perhaps important to note here that wealth production primarily consists in the process of changing, altering and adapting our *material* environment to our needs.) We therefore find, as we could have predicted, that although the assumption is sometimes implicit in those outlooks which come fairly low in the ideological scale, it becomes more and more explicit and frequent as we ascend towards the higher levels – as we move, in other words, towards the extreme Left-wing, and pass through, as it were, those ideologies which increasingly come under the influence of the physical sciences, materialism, and the study of economic evolution.

Another interesting result of our comparative study in respect of the mass-rationality assumption, is the great frequency with which the assumption appears in the statements of a high proportion of scientists, whose work or interest is mainly connected with the mathematical, physical, chemical, biological, technological or economic sciences, and who turn their attention and minds to socio-political matters. As we should be led to expect from theoretical considerations, most of them exhibit or are widely known to have Left-wing sympathies. The occurrence of the assumption is quite rare, however, in the utterances of psychologists and those who have dealings with the study of mental phenomena and development[1].

A few typical examples will illustrate what we mean.

In his book *The German Ideology*, Karl Marx, the famous nineteenth-century economist – founder of scientific socialism, historical and dialectical materialism, and opponent of anarchism – includes a section entitled "The Real Basis of Ideology." This section is mainly occupied with tracing the historical development *of property and the division of labour*, from the Middle Ages down to recent times, and, *on the basis of this analysis*, also with the prediction of the rise "on a mass scale" of the independent mode of thought of the "communist consciousness." (The three sub-sections are entitled "(a) *Intercourse and Productive Power*," "(b) *The Relation of State and Law to Property*" and "(c) *Natural and Civilised Instruments of Production and Forms of Property*.")

Here are some of his words which relate to the mass-rationality assumption:

> Thus things have now come to such a pass, that the individuals must appropriate the existing totality of productive forces, not only to achieve self-activity, but, also, merely to safeguard their very existence. This appropriation is first determined by the object to be appropriated, the productive forces, which have been developed to a totality and which only exist within a universal intercourse. From this aspect alone, therefore, this appropriation must have a universal character corresponding to the productive powers and the inter-course. The appropriation of these powers is itself nothing more than the development of the individual capacities corresponding to the material instruments of production. The appropriation of a totality of instruments of production is, for this very reason, the develop-ment of a totality of capacities in the individuals themselves. This appropriation is further determined by the persons appropriating. Only the proletarians of the present day, who are completely shut off from all self-activity, are in a position to achieve a complete and no longer restricted self-activity, which consists in the appropria-tion of a totality of productive forces and in the thus postulated development of a totality of capacities... In all expropriations up to now, a mass of individuals remain subservient to a single instrument of production; in the appropriation by the proletarians, a mass of instruments of production must be made subject to each individual, and property to all. Modern universal intercourse can be controlled by individuals, therefore, only when controlled by all...Only at this stage does self-activity coincide with material life, which corresponds

---

[1] Jung, for instance, in his *Integration of the Personality*, says: "It is one of the most ridiculous illusions of civilised man that the 'perils of the soul' have entirely disappeared along with primitive superstitions. Even the superstitions have not disappeared from any civilised nation as a whole. They have only changed their names, and often not even that. The din of uprooted intellectual highbrows usually goes on believing in permanent and universal enlightenment. That technical progress and social improvements do not mean psychological differentiation or a higher level of consciousness is a lesson that we are unwilling to learn." (p. 9)

to the development of individuals into complete individuals and the casting-off of all natural limitations...

Finally, from the conception of history we have sketched we obtain these further conclusions: In the development of productive forces there comes a stage at which productive forces and means of intercourse are called into existence, which, under the existing relationships, only cause mischief, and which are no longer productive but destructive forces (machinery and money); and connected with this a class is called forth, which has to bear all the burdens of society without enjoying its advantages, which, ousted from society, is forced into the most decided antagonism to all other classes; a class which forms the majority of all members of society, and from which emanates the consciousness of the necessity of a fundamental revolution, the communist consciousness, which may, of course, arise among the other classes too through the contemplation of the situation of this class... Both for the production on a mass scale of this communist consciousness, and for the success of the cause itself, the alteration of men on a mass scale is necessary, an alteration which can only take place in a practical movement, a *revolution*... (pp. 66-9.)

At the end of the next section – which is headed "Communism: the Production of the Form of Intercourse Itself " we can plainly observe, besides the mass-rationality implication, Marx's emphasis (typical of the intellectual, as we have seen) upon individual assertion as opposed to the collective or group expression (the state):

... The contradiction between the individuality of each separate proletarian and labour, the condition of life forced upon him, becomes evident to him himself, for he is sacrificed from youth upwards and, within his own class, has no chance of arriving at the conditions which would place him in the other class. Thus, while the refugee serfs only wish to be free to develop and assert those conditions of existence which were already there, and hence, in the end, only arrived at free labour, the proletarians, if they are to assert themselves as individuals, will have to abolish the very condition of their existence hitherto (which has, moreover, been that of all society up to the present), namely, labour. Thus they find themselves directly opposed to the form in which, hitherto, individuals have given themselves collective expression, that is, the State. In order, therefore, to assert themselves as individuals, they must overthrow the State. (p. 78.)

We can even detect the assumption in such a statement as the following:

... For as soon as labour is distributed, each man has a particular, exclusive sphere of activity, which is forced upon him and from which he cannot escape. He is a hunter, a fisherman, a shepherd, or a critical critic, and must remain so if he does not want to lose his means of livelihood; while in communist society, where nobody has one exclusive sphere of activity but each can become accomplished in any branch he wishes, society regulates the general production and thus makes it possible for me to do one thing today and another tomorrow, to hunt in the morning, fish in the afternoon, rear cattle in the evening, criticise after dinner, just – as I have a mind, without ever becoming hunter, fisherman, shepherd or critic. (Ibid. p. 22.)

One more sample from Marx exemplifies the assumption even more explicitly:

... From the above it is clear that the real intellectual wealth of the individual depends entirely on the wealth of his real connections. Only then (under communism) will the separate individuals be liberated from the various national and local barriers, be brought into practical connection with the material and intellectual production of the whole world and be put in a position to acquire the capacity to enjoy this all-sided production of the whole earth (the creations of man). Universal dependence, this natural form of the world-historical cooperation of individuals, will be transformed by this communist revolution into the control and conscious mastery of these powers, which, born of the action of men on one another, have till now over awed and governed men as powers completely allied to them. (Ibid. pp. 27-8.)

Another typical extract comes from a chapter entitled "Everyone a Scientist," which forms part of that section of a book, called *Science in the Changing World*, contributed by H. Levy (Professor of Mathematics, Imperial College of Science) whose Left-wing sympathies are well known:

In so far as scientists are people with social ideals, individuals who would like to see the scientific spirit reflected in human development they proceed on the assumption that if only the facts are set out clearly enough people must necessarily accept them...... If education is to fulfill its task it will require to be permeated with the scientific spirit... Every question raised by the child will have to be taken and made an excuse for examining the evidence for the answer given. Throughout its career the child will have to be accustomed to sifting evidence...It is largely a question of early habits. Unless we early instill critical habits into our children, unless we encourage them to call for evidence on all conceivable occasions, they will rapidly adopt a habit of simply *believing*, duly followed by 'believing behaviour...'

... the spirit of science has yet to be liberated for educational service and instilled into social relations. It is a problem that calls for the enterprise and initiative of our generation of teachers and thinkers. By striving to permeate social life with the spirit of critical foresight, by seeking to guide conduct with accurate knowledge, Science may yet carve out a new future for mankind. (pp. 96-106.)

Next, we have a further example from *Let the People Think* by the famous mathematician and writer on relativity physics, Bertrand Russell. In a chapter headed "Can Men be Rational?" he writes:

... Pragmatism emphasises the irrationality of opinion, and psychoanalysis emphasises the irrationality of conduct. Both have led many people to the view that there is no such thing as an ideal of rationality to which opinion and conduct might with advantage conform... I believe such an outlook to be very dangerous, and, in the long run fatal to civilisation...To begin with rationality of opinion: I should define it merely as the habit of taking account of all relevant evidence in arriving at a belief. Where certainty is unobtainable, a rational man will give most weight to the most probable opinion, while retaining others, which have an appreciable probability, in his mind as hypotheses which subsequent evidence may show to be preferable. This, of course, assumes that it is possible in many cases to ascertain facts and probabilities by an objective method – i.e. a method which will lead any two careful people to the same result...... If men were rational, they would take a more correct view of their own interest than they do at present; and if all men acted from enlightened self-interest the world would be a paradise in comparison with what it is...

Rationality in practice may be defined as the habit of remembering all our relevant desires, and not only the one which happens at the moment to be strongest... I believe that all solid progress in the world consists of an increase in rationality, both practical and theoretical... A man is rational in proportion as his intelligence informs and controls his desires. I believe that the control of our acts by our intelligence is ultimately what is of most importance, and what alone will make social life remain possible as science increases the means at our disposal for injuring each other. Education, the press, politics, religion – in a word, all the great forces in the world – are at present on the side of irrationality... The remedy does not lie in anything heroically cataclysmic, but in the efforts of individuals towards a more sane and balanced view of our relations to our neighbours and to the world. It is to intelligence, increasingly widespread, that we must look for the solution of the ills from which our world is suffering. (pp. 14-21.)

A further typical sample is provided by J. B. S. Haldane, F.R.S., Marxist, mathematician, geneticist, and Professor of Biology in the University of London, in his book *The Inequality of Man*:

But science can do something far bigger for the human mind than the substitution of one set of beliefs for another, or the inculcation of scepticism regarding accepted opinions. It can gradually spread among humanity as a whole the point of view that prevails among research workers, and has enabled a few thousand men and a few dozen women to create the science on which modern civilisation rests.

The following characteristic extracts are quoted from *This Changing World*, a symposium written by several well-known scientists and writers, and edited by J. R. M. Brumwell. The first comes from the Editor's Foreword:

... When Darwin publicised evolution it seemed to many both ridiculous and wicked, and directly against what they had been taught in the Bible. Now, less than 100 years afterwards, Darwin's theories are accepted by the general public as common sense and a denial would be thought absurd.

The next appears in Chapter 2, which is entitled "Transformation in Science ," and is contributed by Professor J. D. Bernal, crystallographer, physicist, and equally well known for his Left-wing sympathies and his writings on the relation of science to society:

> One of the paradoxes of the present time is that people may be able to change the world so rapidly that they fail to understand what they are doing. Another is that, while more has been found out at large and in detail about nature and man in the past thirty years than in the whole of history, there is less general appreciation of this knowledge and worse use of it than ever before. This is partly because modern science has become more complex, but as much because it has been professionalised. Since some people are paid to understand it, why should the rest bother their heads about it? But ignorance of science means a failure to understand the factors underlying the critical events of our time. The history of the last few years should have shown that it is no longer optional, but absolutely necessary, for science to be understood, appreciated and effectively used... If people could understand at least something of the possibilities which science offers, they would become more reasonably impatient of their present state, and more capable of changing it. For this science needs to be expounded, and expounded in a new way which emphasises its relation to this changing world. It is no use any longer attempting to present science as a series of pictures of the beauties or the mysteries of the universe and of nature... the scientist must be in close, free and friendly relation with the democratically ordered state machinery, and the people at large must have an adequate understanding of the possibilities and limitations of science... Private and institutional greed, the desire to preserve orders and ranks in a society that has out-grown them, have been potent factors in the past, and are potent factors still, in delaying progress. Unless they are dealt with, and dealt with now, there is no chance for any better world. That is the major practical problem of our time, and it is a social and political one. It will be solved by the people themselves. But the technical forms of the solution, and the rapidity with which it will be possible to achieve a better world, will demand science; and for that reason alone, the people need to know and to understand, possibly better than the scientists themselves, what modern science is, and how it works.

Compare the above words with those which follow, also by Professor Bernal, and which appear in the same chapter:

> Now these great advances (in science) actually incomparably richer than those in the whole previous history of science are also essentially different in character. In recognising them, the scientists have been forced to adopt new mental attitudes which involve a break with the traditions of thought reaching as far back as the Greeks, if not

farther. The simple logic of the schools derived from grammar and commonsense has been found inadequate to cope with the more remote complexities of the atom and the starry universe.We now see that what we call commonsense is just a convenient but crude human tool, suitable enough for a simple life, but needing to be refined and extended to use the new knowledge effectively in a complex situation. It is in respect of its apparent absurdities and contradictions that modern science shows its relation to modern tendencies in art...

Next, we have an excerpt from Chapter 4, "Life from a New Angle," contributed by C. H. Waddington, the well-known biologist – another progressively-minded writer on science and society:

Within the last hundred years, scientific ideas about animals have undergone three revolutions. The first happened in the middle of the last century, and its decisive point was the establishment by Darwin of the theory of evolution. By today this has just about worked through into commonsense. Darwin's contemporaries rejected with horror and disgust the unbiblical idea that human beings are descended from some being much more like an ape than any existing man; but people nowadays have learnt to accept that as a matter of course and to find in it, not a degrading insult, but a reason for hope that we may become still better in the future... Particles and substances are not the fundamental entities into which living things must be analysed: they are only important as parts of processes. It is much more difficult to think like this in actual fact than to say that we ought to do so. Most common-sense methods of picturing the world nowadays are based on the science of the seventeenth century. We 'instinctively' think of solid lumps of stuff, and if they happen to be pushing one another around in some process, that may be interesting but is not essential. In twenty or fifty years' time, or however long it takes for today's science to become 'common-sense,' we shall 'instinctively' think of something going on. If we find it convenient to analyse it into lumps of matter bumping into one another, well and good, but we shall not be surprised if someone else prefers to think of it in some other way. This type of thinking, in terms of processes, is derived from a consideration of the most fundamental and basic properties of living things. We shall therefore have to use it for the ordinary every-day affairs of life as well as for the recondite and far-away matters like the development of a newt's brain... There will still be many kinds of politics; but politics in terms of processes and not of things.It is clear that this kind of thinking is different from our present commonsense. I expect you will be able to find at least hints of the same kind of 'process thinking' in the chapters of the other specialists who contribute to this book.

As final examples from the book, we take the following from J. G. Crowther's Chapters 5 and, 6 headed "Helter Skelter Universe" and "Exploring the Unseeable" respectively. (Mr. Crowther, also Left-wing in outlook, is an authority on the history of science and on science in Soviet Russia, where, in 1930, he was advisor to the Director of Higher Education under the Supreme Economic Council of the U.S.S.R.):

> Professor Bernal tells us in chapter 2 that the whole of human society is passing through enormously important transformations which are occurring far more rapidly than in the past. The pace has quickened. It seems that revolutionary ideas are stirring beneath our thoughts, and are being expressed variously but simultaneously through the imagination of astronomers, poets, physicists, painters and politicians, and will soon become the 'common sense' of the man in the street. (Chapter 5.)... The only means that we have for determining the position of an electron, for showing it up, knocks it from where it was, so we can never be quite sure of its original place. There is a fundamental element of uncertainty in our only means of determining its position. This is the famous Principle of Uncertainty. It is fantastically simple and obvious, but all the genius of Heisenberg was needed to recognise it. This he did by putting the facts into very unfamiliar mathematical dress. He was thus enabled to look at them without any common preconceptions. The greatest achievement of the human mind is to escape from prejudice. When this is done, reality is often found to be quite simple. This in turn happily enables ordinary people to learn the new ideas, until they become the basis of the new common sense. Our grandchildren will find the Principle of Uncertainty as acceptable as the Multiplication Table... The subuniverse of atoms may be chaotic, but it is not unreasonable. If we are willing to invent new mathematical languages, we find we can describe it logically. The new ideas may seem bizarre at first, but we shall soon accept them as normal, just as we shall or do with the new ideas brought forth in painting, music, architecture, politics, and war. (Chapter 6.)

The above examples have been chosen from a multitude – not at random, it is true, but at the same time, without any difficult searching or detailed selective comparison. If, anything, one is almost confronted with an *embarras de choix*. Of course, such statements – containing the mass-rationality assumption – are by no means confined to those physical and biological scientists who apply themselves to politico-ideological matters; they are to be found in the utterances of politicians, doctors, writers and people of almost any trade or profession. Yet nevertheless, after a careful examination, it does appear that, on the whole, the assumption is strongly developed in the social and political outlook of people *in proportion to the extent to which that outlook is influenced by the physico-chemical and biological sciences, or by the philosophy of materialism, which is closely related to these sciences.* This piece of knowledge is further confirmed by the fact that the Left-wing outooks or ideologies often claim to be scientific and tend to adhere, either implicitly or explicitly, to some form of materialist philosophy, which is frequently said to be the "basis" of such an outlook by those holding it.

We have already seen how, by a process of renunciation or repression, the Left-wing (or intellectual) mode of thought becomes differentiated from the mass modes of thinking. But, besides this relation to, or dependence upon, the existence of a mass ideology – the existence, in other words, of the large-scale social group – it would seem that the intellectual mode of thought is also dependent upon a consciousness of its relationship to the physical universe, to the material world at large – in short, upon a philosophy. (It has been well said by Engels, Marx's collaborator, that the central theme or problem of philosophy is the relation of thought to being – of subject to object, mind to matter.) We shall see later, in Part II, how intimately connected are these two relationships – of mind to matter, on the one hand, and of mind to mind, or the group, on the other – and how important they are for understanding the ideological development of the intellect.

But, to return to the above examples of the mass-rationality assumption for a moment, we have another reason for selecting them from the statements of reputable scientists rather than using those from other sources. It is, briefly, that the professional scientist, by virtue of his training, is more definitely committed to the scientific practice and golden rule of demanding that theory, and ideas of things, shall be based on factual evidence, on the study of things as they are and as we actually find them, and not upon what we think things *ought* to be. In the examples quoted, for instance, Professor Levy insists that we "early instill critical habits" and "the scientific spirit" in our children, have them "accustomed to sifting evidence," and "encourage them to call for evidence on all conceivable occasions"; and again, Bertrand Russell defines rationality of opinion as "the habit of taking account of all relevant evidence in arriving at a belief."

When, however, we come to look or "call" for the factual evidence upon which the above statements involving the mass-rationality assumption are founded, in no single case do we find any sign or shred of evidence, or any indication whatever of an objective study of the relevant facts. Indeed, so easily and confidently are these questionable assertions put forward, it would seem that the authors themselves almost regard them as self-evident propositions.

Yet, wherever there is any reference in these statements to *existing* conditions, *to actual fact*, nowhere does it support either the explicit assertion or the implicit assumption of the coming of universal enlightenment and mass-rationality.

In the last quotation from Marx, for example, he refers (when speaking of group or "universal" dependence) to "these powers, which, born of the action of men on one another, have till now overawed and governed men as powers completely alien to them." And nearly a hundred years later, we note, Levy, Russell, Bernal and Waddington are saying much the same thing. In Professor Levy's statement quoted above, he says "the spirit of science is yet to be liberated for educational service and instilled into social relations. It is a problem that calls for the enterprise and initiative of our generation of teachers and thinkers." Bertrand Russell, we see, states that "Education, the press, politics, religion – in a word, all the great forces in the world – are at present on the side of irrationality." Again, Professor Bernal states above that "while more has been found out at large and in detail about nature and man in the past thirty years than in the whole of history, there is less general appreciation of this knowledge and worse use of it than ever before." And, in speaking above of scientific "process thinking" which, he asserts, will become universal, we observe C. H. Waddington says: "it is much more difficult to think like this in actual fact than to say that we ought to do so... It is clear that this kind of thinking is different from our present commonsense."

Thus, in the face of this patent lack of evidence for the mass-rationality implication, we are in the position of having to account for the assumption of the coming of universal enlightenment on the part of trained scientists who, not only are themselves accustomed to demanding evidence "on all conceivable occasions" but who urge everybody else to do the same, and moreover, who insist, because everyone "ought" or "must," that they *will* eventually do the same. Has this curious paradoxical situation anything to do with the paradoxical state of social affairs that we introduced at the beginning of this book? It may seem rather remote at the moment but we venture to think that it may have. For, as we have suggested earlier, the mass-rationality assumption is to be found, not only rooted in the ideologies of the extreme Left, but also, with widely varying degrees of explicitness, *underlying every democratic outlook*. As James Burnham has remarked, in *The Managerial Revolution*, it is "important to observe that no major ideology is content to profess openly that it speaks only for the group whose interests it in fact expresses. Each group insists that its ideologies are universal in validity and express the interests of humanity as a whole; and each group tries to win universal acceptance for its ideologies." This observation applies less to fascism, perhaps, than to any other political outlook, but it certainly is true of every democratic ideology.

We can find the mass-rationality assumption in the anarchist, communist, socialist and liberal outlooks and we can even detect its beginnings in democratic conservatism, though perhaps not so consistently, and in a more primitive and implicit form. Take these statements, for instance, from Baldwin's *On England* (1926):

> That appalling twopenny-ha'penny gift of fluency, with the addition of a certain amount of training and of imagination in word-spinning, is the kind of rhetoric which stirs the emotions of the ignorant mob and sets it moving. It is because such forces can be set in motion by rhetoric that I have no regard for it, but a positive horror. Very rarely do we find the gift given to men who have wisdom and constructive power, and for the time being it would seem that it was in this world a force far beyond its merits, although in the more advanced countries I sometimes hope that it is past its prime. At least I believe that in England and Scotland at any rate rhetoric of the kind I have tried to describe no longer makes that appeal to the people.I think it may be that the people of this country are getting just the least bit suspicious of the literary rhetoric of our Sunday Press, and of our daily Press, and that this very wholesome dread, this wholesome nervousness, is being transferred from the Press to the platform. I think that throughout this country there is today a far greater desire than there has ever been before to hear plain, unadorned statements of cases. I believe that anyone who has taken part in recent elections – a few constituencies excepted – will agree with me that one of the most remarkable features is the way in which large audiences all over the country will listen to a statement of a case, whether they agree with it or not, provided they feel that the statement is made honestly and fairly, and with due consideration for the opposite view. (pp. 101-2)

Now if the mass-rationality assumption has no objective foundation, as we may justifiably suspect from our brief study of groups – firstly from the study of mass groups, and secondly, from the study of the emergence of the intellectual from such groups – if, in other words, we question the validity of the mass-rationality implication, we shall, I venture to suggest, begin to see quite a lot of social and political phenomena from a new angle and in a new light. Certain events, previously inexplicable or inadequately or only partly explained, begin to take on a new shape, to sort themselves out and to assume a more intelligible significance. Events which previously seemed more or less remote from each other and unrelated, come together and exhibit close relationship.

But here, we must remind the reader, it must be carefully and clearly borne in mind just what it is we are questioning. It is important to realise that we are not calling into question the capacity of the masses to acquire knowledge or to extend their knowledge as such; we are not even questioning their capacity to increase, as such, their rationality – that is to say, to extend their existing level of rationality over a broader field. We have already seen (Chapter 2) that we must distinguish between the quantitative (or horizontal) development of the intellect and its qualitative (its vertical or ideological) development. We have also seen that some members of the mass groups may have a large degree of intelligence or, in same cases, even a larger degree of intelligence; than is possessed by the average member of an intellectual group of higher qualitative development. Every act of knowing or understanding, we shall see, immediately involves two essential conditions (1), the thing or fact which is to be known and (2), a mode of thought, or system or way of thinking, appropriate to the nature of the type of fact which is to be known. (We shall find inadequate the more common conception of knowing, which stresses the fact to be known (or environment) and regards the mind as a mere inert receptacle somewhat like a pint-pot, or as a passive reflector like a mirror, and as making no positive contribution to the finished product of the knowing process. The quotation given above from Levy exemplifies this inadequate conception on the part of certain scientists, where he says: "In so far as scientists are people with social ideals... they proceed on the assumption that if only the facts are set out clearly enough people must necessarily accept them...")

When we question the mass-rationality assumption, what we are doubting is, not whether the masses are capable of developing or extending their existing made of thought (i.e. quantitatively), but whether they are capable, *as a mass*, of developing the qualitatively higher modes of thought – of exchanging, in short, their existing mode for the independent, analytic ideological mode of the scientific intellectuals, same of whom, according to Bernal (see above) "have been forced to adapt new mental attitudes which involve a break with the traditions of thought reaching as far back as the Greeks, if not farther." (Note also Bernal's further statement: "The simple logic of the schools derived from grammar and commonsense has been found inadequate to cope with the more remote complexities of the atom and the starry universe... what we call common sense is just a convenient but crude human tool, suitable enough far a simple life...")

Science, it has been well said, is born in scepticism. And we have said that if we begin to doubt the mass-rationality assumption – as, in view of our preliminary study, we are so entitled to do – then certain events will start to take an a new significance, and certain apparently unconnected events can be related together mare than has been possible hitherto.

To illustrate, take the case already referred to (p.52) – and described in detail by Chakotin in *The Rape of the Masses* – of the rejection, in Germany, in 1932, by the Left-wing leadership, of the proposal to introduce on a large scale, what Chakotin calls "senso-propaganda" (scientific but violently emotional propaganda) into the Left-wing's struggle with the Nazis far popular support and consequent power. As we have stated earlier, the new scientific methods were tried out an a comparatively small scale with great success. In his book, Chakatin publishes in full the report an the situation by the person – a competent and far-seeing individual – what, at the time, was in charge of anti-Nazi propaganda. The report is well worth diligent study and, in our opinion at least, is a very important and significant document. We can only reproduce here sufficient to show its relevance and make our point:

> The new methods of combat by means of symbols (the three arrows, the clenched fist, the shout of 'Freedom!') had been proposed and had undergone their first test in the streets of Heidelberg, with very encouraging results, and the real struggle had now to be entered on... I sent a plan of propaganda to Berlin. But I waited in vain for a reply... After waiting a fortnight I received from Berlin, a few days before the elections, the reply that "it will be made use of if necessary" at the second ballot. I sent the whole system of symbols, with concrete, detailed plans of propaganda and organisation, to Berlin, but received no further reply. During this campaign the party propaganda was developed very slowly, and could not claim to be on a par with that of the other side either in quantity or quality. Once more our tracts proved too long and too doctrinaire; they could not be read without yawning. Two or three clumsy posters, unimaginative and uninspiring, were to be seen on the walls; they showed figures of misery, groaning and lamenting, and talking with anguish of the approach of the Third Reich. Was not this simple madness, a convincing proof of entire lack of psychological intuition? Was it not actually serving Hitler's cause? While he uttered his threats, our posters gave them concrete form, thus carrying on a propaganda of intimidation in the wrong direction. People were going to our party meetings, but what could they get there? Interminable speeches, historical statements, figures and statistics, and argumentation, relieved from time to time with rather vulgar jests and witticisms. The most active of our comrades were wasting their time on insignificant meetings in tiny centres. I put before one of our party secretaries, a man who was exhausting himself in this sort of "activity," the following calculation: at the height of the electoral campaign, with the Nazi propaganda making progress like wild-fire, with the Nazis masters of the streets, displaying their symbols everywhere, falling upon our followers and starting street-fights, our leader had left the town to speak in some hole to a hundred people, of whom about eighty were with us already and would have voted for us in any case. We could not hope to win over more than half of the remaining twenty. To this end, to get ten votes, he had left the offices of the party, left young members who were burning to help kicking their heels

at home, and left the comrades of the *Reichsbanner* to wander aimlessly about the streets; for he had sent the local leaders of the *Reichsbanner* and the local youth leaders to speak in similar holes. The same spectacle was to be seen everywhere.But all my plans for activity, for modernising our fighting methods, were met by secretaries and officials of the party with the invariable reply: 'We can do nothing without instructions from the central committee in Berlin.' In desperation, I decided to act on my own initiative; who could forbid me to use my energies as a member of the party?

I spent two days visiting the principal centres in south and south-west Germany... I had the good fortune to win over some active men among the secondary leaders; the younger members, especially, adopted the new methods with enthusiasm and thereafter vigorously carried them into execution... Party secretaries and leaders of the *Reichsbanner* in these: towns told me of the jubilant enthusiasm that had taken hold of our young militants and the ardour with which they rushed into the propagandist melee...

I was satisfied: the new method of propaganda had undergone its trial by fire; this was reported to me from all parts in the south of Germany... The report on the effect on our opponents was always the same – 'disconcerted,' 'taken aback,' 'in perplexity.' All the newspapers of the middle class wrote of the sudden activity of the masses of the Iron Front.

On the other hand, reports soon began to come in of difficulties and dissension within our organisations. There were differences of opinion between the leaders of the *Reichsbanner*, those of the Iron Front, and those of the Social Democratic Party. I had foreseen the danger of this, and had at once tried to get into touch with the principal party leaders, to awaken their interest and to enlist their sympathy for the new ideas... But I failed entirely. The party direction refused to organise a conference at which I might have explained my aims; the high officials of the party remained invisible – they were always speaking all over the Reich, and there was in reality no methodically organised central direction; as for a plan of campaign, nobody was bothering about it. The so-called central recruiting bureau, in charge of all propaganda and of the distribution of posters and tracts, was run by men with no experience of political propaganda and not the slightest comprehension of its principles. I tried to talk to them, to get into discussion with them, but it was labour in vain... These officials had heard of my lecture, but they felt certain objections of principle; they had no great opinion of psychology or of any science of politics. To my great distress, I now saw clearly, for the first time, that here I was powerless...

... We worked unremittingly in our central propaganda bureau. But soon I noticed signs of weariness, coming, as usual, from the higher ranks... Otto Horsing suddenly reappeared in the *Reichsbanner* offices. He was the leader of that organisation, but had not been seen for some time. Now he had come back – to work against the new ideas. They were 'too modern,' 'too dangerous,' they were contrary to police regulations (textitsic!) what was more, they seemed to him to be ridiculous, and to expose us to the risk of being 'misunderstood' by the public. He demanded that all further development of the new propaganda should be suspended...

What was to be done? There was not a day to lose in the struggle against the Hitlerist menace, but everything had to be begun again from the beginning. My task, above all, was to carry on propaganda in our ranks in favour of propaganda... There was thus only one thing to do – to try to convince the leaders... I tried to persuade each of them personally – Vogel, Breitscheid, Hilferding, Herts, Grassman, Kiinstler, Heilmann, Lobe, Stampfer, and others. I went to see them, talked with them for whole hours, and tried hard to convince them from figures, diagrams, and maps... But when they came together in committee they all rejected the new ideas. They sent me to perdition, especially Otto Wels, the great leader of the party, and all his speeches ended with the statement that since he was against these ideas it was a waste of time to talk about them.

The only thing, then, was to beard him, no light task. I knew in advance that he was entirely against our new propaganda. At first he had refused to listen to the idea of a campaign by means of symbols. His arguments were entirely incredible in the mouth of the leader of a revolutionary party – 'We shall make ourselves ridiculous with all this nonsense.'

Thus, we can see that the collapse of the Left-wing movement in Germany, in the face of the rising tide of fascism, was in part at least, due to the failure of its propaganda to win popular support – a propaganda which, it must be emphasised, was largely determined by doctrinaire leaders and intellectuals, and consequently, *mainly based on the mass-rationality assumption.*

Another illustration of the heuristic value in questioning that validity of the mass-rationality assumption is the case of Soviet Russia, where, during the 1918 Revolution, the Left-wing Bolsheviks, by supporting and urging the popular demands of the long-oppressed, but illiterate and mainly non-political, peasants – "Peace, Bread and Land!" – captured state power. After more than a quarter of a century of almost unlimited political power – during which time all political opposition to the official Communist Party has been ruthlessly suppressed and the Russian communists have tried continuously to impose their communist ideology upon the masses – religion, superstition, nationalism, hero-worship, patriotism, love of symbolism, militarism, authority, hierarchy, etc., etc., in short, the typical characters of the mass ideology, still obstinately persist among the Russian people; and moreover, the evidence from Russia of recent years tends to show that these characteristic features of the mass ideology are gaining more and more open expression. Again, the membership of the Communist Party of Russia still remains a tiny minority of the whole Russian population, whereas, by contrast, the membership of the German Nazi Party at the height of its power embraced a relatively larger proportion of the German people.

Many other problems connected with social development and events – notably, for instance, the paradoxical state of affairs, described in Chapter 1, in which science produces for man the means of controlling his material environment but is quite impotent in supplying him with the means to control his human environment – begin to wear a less puzzling aspect in the light of our new scepticism of the scientific intellectual's assumption that mankind *as a whole* is moving towards the ideological homogeneity of mass rationality, towards the analytic, objective and independent mode of thought. Lack of space prevents the detailed enumeration and analysis of these other problems here, but enough has been said, we suggest, to warrant the continued pursuit of our inquiry along the lines indicated by the present, tentative results of our study. In Part II of this book we shall endeavour to come to some understanding of the underlying mechanisms of ideological and political development, particularly with the idea of tracing, if possible, the psycho-biological origin of the mass-rationality assumption.

Meanwhile, we may reflect that, if human society is not moving towards ideological homogeneity – which is the implication of the mass-rationality assumption – but if, as we suspect, it is moving towards ideological heterogeneity (and it has already developed considerably heterogeneity in this respect) then we shall have the full weight of the evidence of universal evolution to support us. The following words are taken from Herbert Spencer's *First Principles*, the famous work in which he shows by a mass of evidence that progressive differentiation, or advance from homogeneity to heterogeneity, is a general characteristic or law of evolution:

> Advance from the homogeneous to the heterogeneous is clearly displayed in the progress of the latest and most heterogeneous creature – Man. While the peopling of the Earth has been going on, the human organism has grown more heterogeneous among the civilised divisions of the species; and the species, as a whole, has been made more heterogeneous by the multiplication of races and the differentiation of them from one another... On passing from Humanity under its individual form to Humanity as socially embodied, we find the general law still more variously exemplified. The change from the homogeneous to the heterogeneous is displayed equally in the progress of civilisation as a whole, and in the progress of every tribe or nation; and it is still going on with increasing rapidity.Society in its first and lowest stage is a homogeneous assemblage of individuals having like powers and like functions: the only marked difference of function being that which accompanies difference of sex. Every man is warrior, hunter, fisherman, tool-maker, builder; every woman performs the same drudgeries; every family is self-sufficing, and, save for purposes of companionship, aggression, and defence, might as well live apart from the rest. Very early, however, in the course of social evolution, we find an incipient differentiation between the governing and the governed... Not only is the law thus exemplified in the evolution of the social organism, but it is exemplified in the evolution of all products of human thought and action, whether concrete or abstract, real or ideal... The advance from the simple to the complex, through successive modifications upon modifications, is seen alike in the earliest changes of the Heavens to which we can reason our way back, and in the earliest changes we can in-

ductively establish; it is seen in the geologic and climatic evolution of the Earth, of every individual organism on its surface and in the aggregate of organisms; it is seen in the evolution of Humanity, whether contemplated in the civilised man, or in the assemblage of races; it is seen in the evolution of Society, in respect alike of its political, its religious, and its economical organisation; and it is seen in the evolution of those countless concrete and abstract products of human activity, which constitute the environment of our daily life. From the remotest past which Science can fathom, up to the novelties of yesterday, an essential trait of Evolution has been the transformation of the homogeneous into the heterogeneous.

Another general characteristic of evolution, dwelt upon at length by Spencer, and upon which we can reflect in connection with the ideological development of man, is the progressive integration of mutually-dependent parts which accompanies the transformation of homogeneity into heterogeneity. Human society began its development as a more or less loose collection or assemblage of individuals (with no great degree of mutual dependence except in relation to the sex function) very much in the same manner as the animal body began its evolution as a loose, homogeneous assemblage (colony) of individual cells; and, just as in the evolution of the animal, there occurs an increasing specialisation and integration of function among groups of individual cells – and consequently, an increasing dependence of these groups upon one another – so, similarly, does human society exhibit in its development, an increasing specialisation and integration of function among groups of individual members of society. In the same way that the animal body, in the course of its evolution, gradually develops into a more and more self-regulating, self-controlled organism, so does human society; and, as in the case of the animal, different groups of cells become related in different ways to the whole mechanism of the economy, regulation and control of the organism, and form a series of levels of function – a hierarchy of functions – so, we suggest, in the case of human society, different ideological groups of individuals become related in different ways to the whole mechanism of the economics, regulation and control (or government) of the social organism, and form a similar hierarchy of functions.

Yet another general characteristic of the evolutionary process which relates to our study of the ideological structure and development of society, is the coexistence, within an integrating system, of many levels of development; and moreover, their coexistence in such a manner that, where the qualitatively higher levels depend for their existence upon the existence of the lower levels, these lower levels are represented by a greater number of unit – parts or members than are the higher levels. This characteristic can be seen, for example, in the numerical preponderance of protons and electrons over atoms, in the numerical preponderance of atoms over molecules, in that of inorganic molecules over organic molecules, of organic molecules over cells, of unicellular organisms over multicellular organisms, and so on. The principle applies equally well to the levels of function exhibited in the structure of a single individual organism (such as an atom, molecule, cell or animal body) or to those same levels exhibited externally in the universe at large. The ideological structure of human society and the evolution of ideologies exhibit this same general characteristic, namely, in that the lower levels of the ideological scale, from which the higher layers have developed, are represented by a greater number of individual members than are the higher layers. Finally, the principle also applies – as we shall see more clearly in Part II – to the ideas appropriate to the different levels of ideological development exhibited in the mental structure of a single individual.

Part II

Ideological Structure
and Development

2.1 The Ideological Field

The life of the contemporary spirit is a cycle of stages, which on the one hand still have a synchronous co-existence, and only from another view appear as a sequence in time that has passed. The experiences which the spirit seems to have behind it, exists also in the depths of its present being.

– Hegel, *The Philosophy of History*
(quoted in Mannheim's *Ideology and Utopia*)

In the development of consciousness, which at first sight appears limited to the point of form merely, there is thus at the same time included the development of the matter or of the objects discussed in the special branches of philosophy. But the latter process must, so to speak, go on behind consciousness, since those facts are the essential nucleus which is raised into consciousness.

– Hegel, *The Science of Logic*

IT is so familiar a circumstance, and it seems so natural to us, for people to differ in their opinions, that it may appear somewhat odd to ask why it is so, or to inquire what it is that determines a person's set of beliefs, or what causes them to grow, change or persist. People, living together, working together, often leading the same kind of life – sometimes members of the same family – quite commonly display the most divergent views on many issues of religion, politics, art, morals and so forth. How often have we not heard of two such people that they cannot agree on any one subject?

Deep divergencies of opinion surround us on all sides; from the press, pulpit, radio, screen, public platform and hoarding proceeds a vast and diverse mass of conflicting ideas; minor or major controversies and differences of opinion are continually raging in the home, the street, the park, the public house, the restaurant, the meeting hall and in parliament itself. Think of the almost innumerable "pro" and "anti" societies, leagues, associations, movements, parties, federations, unions, sects, denominations and the like, each of them standing for, and organised to further, a particular set of ideas. Think, too, of the immense number of pamphlets, books and journals devoted to particular causes and crusades of one kind or another. Ideas of every sort and description are the constant environment of the inhabitants of a modern civilised community.

One might think that this veritable plethora of contrasting ideas and attitudes was a rich field and hunting ground for scientific study. Yet, so used are we to this bewildering multiciplicity of ideas, that most of us take it all for granted and never pause to question how it is that people come to be thus divided, or grouped together against each other, in the way they are. What causes people to become ardent or passionate protagonists of certain ideas? What makes them so emphatic or vehement about some ideas and not about others? What makes men die for an idea? We are so familiar with the phenomenon of vehemency that we rarely question how it arises or what sustains it. Frequently it is dismissed with such phrases as "Oh!

he has a bee in his bonnet," "he's got a slight kink when it comes to that subject" or "he's now on his hobby-horse." Why are most people, particularly the older ones, so difficult to shift in their opinions? How do beliefs, opinions and understanding originate? How do people become "interested" in an idea or set of ideas? What is "interest" and the mechanisms underlying it? Are there independent laws peculiar to and governing the growth of intellect? If so what are they? Is there any close connection between ideologies and understanding? What determines a person's ideas or his outlook on life?

Such questions are rarely asked. If we could answer them in scientific terms the answers would, we venture to suggest, have an important bearing on such practical matters as education and training, propaganda and publicity, relations between social groups, industrial and political cooperation, international cooperation and relations – and, through these, on the great problem of the self-control of human society, of man's control of that part of his environment constituted by himself.

Of the comparative few who do give these questions any consideration, the majority come to a variety of conflicting, quickly-arrived-at and very general conclusions. Some take the realm of ideas more or less at its face value and regard a person's beliefs as due almost entirely to chance and accident or to Divine Providence. Some think that people's opinions are basically determined by biological factors – hereditary qualities, instincts, reflexes, glandular conditions etc. – which are said to decide the extent, or limit, of a person's outlook and insight into the nature of things. Some assure us that beliefs are fundamentally determined by economic interests and conditions. Others tell us that all ideas are ultimately reducible to physico-chemical processes or to the motions of material particles, and are therefore ultimately governed by the laws of physics and dynamics. Some combine these explanations in various ways; still others refer us for enlightenment to other fields of study, such as that of psychology, which, though it has many branches, is still largely confined to the study of perception and feeling. But practically all come to an end of their inquiries, and rest content with these (or some such) rather simple generalisations. The one thing about which most of those who regard the problem at all appear to be agreed – implicitly at least – is the futility of seriously studying the actual sphere or field of ideas, beliefs, opinions, theories etc. *itself*. Rather, it never or rarely occurs to them that such a study is possible, or if possible, could lead to fruitful and useful results. Few indeed are they who even suspect that the sphere of ideologies possesses scientifically intelligible relations, properties, processes and laws of its own.

It is as though we were to dispense with the study of the *interrelations* of, say, economic or sociological phenomena, and endeavour to account for these phenomena in terms of a study of the biological field – in terms of biological laws and processes. Or, again, it is as if we were to disregard the *internal* study of the biological field and merely regard the biological phenomena in purely physico-chemical terms. Apropos of this latter, the biologist J. B. S. Haldane, has said: "... the basic principles of physics are not of such a nature as to force him (the physiologist) to the view that because an organism in its details observes physical and chemical laws, therefore it must be a machine... the organism is something more than a machine, in the sense that it has a unity of a type which the machine lacks." Similarly with ideological phenomena, which, although they are conditioned by physical, chemical, biological and sociological laws and processes, nevertheless possess internal relations and exhibit laws of a type which is peculiar to them. No doubt the very richness of contrast and diversity, the apparent impermanence, the apparently unlimited extent and the intangibility of the ideological material, which make it seem beyond the power of science to handle, has something to do with this negative attitude towards the domain of ideologies. But that is not the whole story. For, as we shall see, there exists a definite prejudice – rarely voiced but implicit in the outlook of most people – which regards the constituents and relations of the ideological domain as intrinsically capricious and chaotic in their essential nature; and this would imply that we are incapable of successfully applying scientific or rational methods to the understanding of this particular realm.

The attitude is in many ways comparable with the attitude of the child, or that of the savage mentality, to the surrounding world of material objects. As is well known, children and primitive people project their own feelings, their own subjectivity and capriciousness, into the outer world. They people their material environment with erratic, refractory spirits and thus attempt to account for the unmanageable world of matter by referring it to the capricious world of ideas (objectivity is referred to subjectivity). As man's knowledge grows, and scientific understanding conquers and occupies one territory after another, the whimsical spirits are gradually, stage by stage, driven back from the world of matter towards their original home and last refuge: the domain of ideas and ideologies. In the meantime, from its simple beginnings, this ancient stronghold of caprice has grown and changed nearly out of all recognition. It has become a large territory and developed a vast, unwieldy population. Throughout the domain as a whole there is apparently no recognised organisation or system of law and order, and anarchy appears to reign supreme.

Because of the lack of a recognised and understood system of law and order in this realm – and consequent absence of any technique of control – its inhabitants are getting out of hand and threaten to become still more unmanageable. In the words of McDougall, in his *World Chaos*:

> The top-heaviness of our civilisation is due to the rapid development
> of Science; its lop-sidedness is due to the lop-sidedness of our Science.
> Our civilisation reflects the state of our knowledge; and especially it
> reflects it faithfully in respect of the lop-sided state of our Science...
> Since the time of Galileo, Physical Science, by which I mean the
> sciences of the inorganic or physical realm, has advanced at a
> constantly accelerating pace. The Sciences of life have lagged far
> behind... we talk of psychology, of economics and of political science,
> of jurisprudence, of sociology and of many other supposed sciences;
> but the simple truth is that all these fine names simply mark great
> gaps in our knowledge, or rather fields of possible sciences that as
> yet have hardly begun to take shape and being. The names stand for
> aspirations rather than achievements; they define a programme, they
> vaguely indicate regions of a vast wilderness hardly yet explored, and
> certainly not mapped, regions in which chaos still reigns, yet *regions*
> *which must be reduced to order if our civilisation is to endure...*
> lack of understanding and control of the human and social factors
> of our civilisation lags far behind our material development and
> renders negatory, and even gravely injurious, advances in physical

knowledge and control which might be of the greatest benefit to
all the world... we need the development of the Social Sciences,
economics, politics, jurisprudence, criminology, penology, history,
social anthropology, and all the rest, for our guidance in all social
and political problems, in face of all of which we stumble blindly
along amidst a chaos of conflicting opinions. And all of these need
for their foundation some sure knowledge of the constitution of
human nature and of the principles of its development...

Thus, we can discern the urgency and importance of the need to come to some
understanding of the ideological nature and development of man. For man's intellect,
though it has mastered a great deal of the universe which is its environment, has
not mastered itself. This is the great paradox of our time. Hence the need for
systematised knowledge of the ideological field, a science of ideologies – a science
which must of necessity revolve around the central problem of understanding man's
mental development, of understanding *understanding*.

2.2 Definition of Ideology

BEFORE we go on to describe the typical course of ideological development and attempt to come to some understanding of its underlying mechanisms, it will be necessary to get some clearer idea of what we mean by the word "ideology." This will demand a discussion of two important and leading concepts which are indispensable for the clear comprehension of our meaning of the term. They are, firstly, the concept of "assumption," and, secondly, the concept of "identification."

According to the *Concise Oxford Dictionary* the word "ideology" means "the science of ideas, also; visionary speculation." We shall be unconcerned with the second of these two interpretations of the term, but in addition to the above definitions, the *Addenda* of the same dictionary gives the following: "(also) ideas at the basis of some economic or political theory or system: (*Nazi, Fascist, ideology*)." Now, although we shall sometimes use the word with approximately the same meaning as the first definition given above, we wish at the moment to draw special attention to this last definition; Thus, our use of the term "ideology" will be similar to the dual use of such a term as, say, "morphology," which means (a), the science or study of organic forms and structures, and (b), the form of structure of an organism.

The more frequent sense in which we shall use the word "ideology" undoubtedly approximates to the last interpretation – that given in the *Addenda* of the dictionary – which definition however, as it stands, is too rigid and arbitrarily restricted to suit our present purposes. For example, the dictionary confines the term to the basic ideas underlying some system of economic or political theories. We shall therefore find it convenient to extend this definition to include the basic ideas (or rather, the assumptions) underlying any system of ideas. And since we shall find that all ideas (or more definitely, all propositions) are based on, or take for granted, certain cognitive assumptions, and that, moreover, on the basis of these assumptions, propositions can be classified or divided into groups or systems, then it can be seen that our extended definition will cover the whole field of propositions – political, economic, religious, philosophical, scientific or otherwise.

This extension of the meaning of "ideology" may at first seem rather too broad, but upon further consideration I think we shall find that the removal of the rather arbitrary limitation attached to the ordinary meaning is not only desirable but necessary for clear thinking, and is of great practical value. Without necessarily defining it, quite a number of writers in recent years have tended to use the term much as we shall use it in this wider, but more objective, sense. However, we have by no means exhausted what we are to understand by an ideology and we must consider the matter further.

Besides the *cognitive aspect* – the logically implied assumptions – there is another and equally important aspect to be taken into account in defining an ideology, since it is an essential and necessary ingredient, characteristic of all ideologies. It is, namely, the emotional or *affective* aspect – that aspect which is connected with morals, values etc. – and we may consider it as complementary to, and as mutually interpenetrating with, the cognitive aspect. Using a very crude analogy, we can say that the affective element is the mortar which binds the bricks of the cognitive element together to form a whole. Just as the cognitive aspect of an ideology is characterised by a particular set of logically implied assumptions, so, similarly, the affective aspect is characterised by a particular set of emotional ties or "identifications." These identifications – which vary in their strength from one ideological group to another, and from person to person in the same ideological group – attach themselves to a whole range of things: from general assumptions, abstract principles and ideas, to concrete facts, forms, symbols, and even particular objects or persons. Each set of identifications – and every human being possesses such a set – forms a kind of "scale of values" – a phrase sometimes used in common parlance, and under which this affective aspect of an ideology is more popularly known or recognised.

We shall find that in an ideology there are involved two kinds of cognitive assumptions – positive and negative – and equally, that there are involved two kinds of emotional identification – positive and negative identifications. Negative assumptions are implied in the denial of certain propositions, and negative identifications are implied by the emotional repudiation or rejection of certain ideas, things or persons. We shall find, too, that these two aspects of an ideology (cognitive and affective) to some extent interact with and condition each other – which indicates, at one and the same time, some measure of independence of each other and also their mutual inter-dependence. Thus these two aspects of an ideology may and do interact also, partly independently and partly together, *as two aspects of an individual's mental organisation*, with the environment of the individual. Again, we shall find that these two aspects grew out of one another by a kind of fission-process, or, to put it another way, became differentiated from a more or less homogeneous condition, an original mental state, which we shall call "self-identification."

Now, it will be noticed upon examination that our conception of an ideology has undergone or is undergoing a somewhat radical change: upon a merely static conception of an ideology, as composed of a number of set "ideas at the basis of some economic or political theory or system" – of itself a rather barren and rigid conception – we have superimposed certain ideas which give to our original concept a dynamic character. An ideology, which previously was a more or less empty, abstract husk or shell, largely removed from the life of the individual and actual mental events, has now become more a conception of a living, growing thing, and intimately connected with the mental life of every human being; our conception of an ideology has, from a vague concept of something relating to a mere arbitrary collection of abstract ideas, fixed and remote from the living person, become an actual, growing, changing state of each human being's mental organisation. This change – from static to more dynamic and concrete conceptions is a characteristic feature in the evolution of thought and of science, and, as it comes within the province of ideological development, we shall learn more of it in later pages.

When we think of an ideology in this more dynamic sense, we mean much the same thing as that when we use such expressions as "outlook on life," "general attitude of mind," "mode of thought," "intellectual position," "*Weltanschauung*," "mental standpoint," "method of approach," "general viewpoint" and so on. A good illustration of this is the title of C. H. Waddington's interesting book, *The Scientific Attitude*, a book in which he seeks to describe the ideology (in our sense) of science. Waddington says in the foreword (note the reference to the affective aspect of the scientist's "attitude to the world"): "I shall argue that science can not only solve special technical problems, such as the correct amount of vitamins to have in our bread, but that it has also developed an attitude to the world which make some things seem valuable and others not; and these standards of the scientific world cannot be overlooked when the general problem of values is being discussed."

Our revised, more dynamic and concrete conception of an ideology may now be defined as the complete system of cognitive assumptions and affective identifications which manifest themselves in, or underlie, the thought, speech, aims, interests, ideals, ethical standards, actions – in short, in the behaviour – of an individual human being. The definition is, of course, broad and not a final one; like all definitions it will be subject to greater determination as we fill in the details and our knowledge and understanding grow more determinate.

It will be clear from our new definition that everyone has an ideology, since everyone, however primitive, has some kind of emotional and intellectual life which expresses itself in his or her behaviour. In fact, as I think can easily be shown, we are all born with the primitive beginnings of an ideology – beginnings which we have partly inherited and partly acquired *in utero*. It seems likely, too, from our definition, that no two individuals will have *exactly* and *precisely* the same ideology, i.e., exactly the same detailed structure of cognitive assumptions and affective identifications. They will differ in this respect much as they differ anatomically and physiologically; that is to say, some structural details will be present in one but not in another, and other characteristics will be present in two or more but will differ in form or degree.

Yet, while each individual ideology may differ from all others – as every animal's morphology or structure differs in some way from that of every other animal – we shall find, as in the case of fauna, broad resemblances and common features which enable us to classify them into related groups. It follows, then, that before we can classify ideologies into groups according to their likenesses and differences we have to know something of their structures – which structures must be, for our purpose, more or less permanent; and we shall find that, like the physiological structure of an organism, while the details are constantly changing, growing and decaying, the main parts of the ideological structure remain more or less the same.

How are we to discover and analyse the structure of the ideology of an individual? Broadly speaking, *by studying his behaviour, but more particularly, by studying that part of his behaviour which largely arises from, or manifests, his conscious intentions* (this aspect of human behaviour tends to be excluded from the field of psychology – a science which rather confines itself to the study of the more automatic or involuntary aspects of behaviour). Although intentional or voluntary behaviour may include such forms as locomotion, movements of the limbs, etc., it is to the form of speech – or more properly, the spoken or written utterance of thought that we must turn for the study of the most direct expression of an individual's conscious intentions. In other words, in order to study the ideology of a person, we must mainly study *what* he says and also the *manner* in which it is said; also, we must make a comparative study of the utterances of this person with the utterances of others. But it does not mean that we have to examine *every* utterance of this or that particular individual. For, once we know the "materials" of which an ideology is composed – that is to say, cognitive assumptions and affective identifications, the bricks and mortar of our analogy – once we know what we are to look for, as well as where we are to look for them, then we shall find that the broad structure of the ideology (or part of it) can often be detected in a relatively small sample of utterance, especially if it happens to be of the right kind. It will naturally vary from one person to another.

While the ideology or "outlook" of an individual shows its influence in practically all his conduct – though this, too, varies considerably – it manifests itself, as may be expected, more directly in that part of his conduct which is less directly determined by his *immediate* environment. To make this clearer, we can usefully regard the different forms of human behaviour (using the word "behaviour" in its widest possible sense) after the manner of an ascending scale or graded, hierarchic system of levels: where the more palpable or readily perceived forms of behaviour at the lower end are predominantly determined by immediate mechanical and physical agencies – as in the case, for example, of the influence of gravity, atmospheric pressure and temperature, etc., upon the condition, position and movement of the body, either in part or as a whole; where, rising in the scale, the forms of behaviour such as involve the natural bodily functions are largely determined by the chemical and biological processes of the body; and where, in the higher levels, the less palpable forms of behaviour – which involve acquired functions and abilities, expression of instincts, emotions, moral attitudes, logical thought etc. – are largely influenced by psychological and ideological processes. It will be noticed that, as we ascend the scale, each succeeding level – although involving processes of all the levels below it, and moreover, including them as parts of itself – is associated with progressively less of the material structure of the body.

The processes of each level influence *all* the behaviour throughout the whole scale of levels, though variably – that is: either more, or less directly. Gravity, for instance, influences the state and position of the whole body *directly* or immediately, but it influences a person's ideas *indirectly* or mediately, which is to say, per medium of the processes of other levels, e.g., biological, psychological and ideological processes. Likewise, ideological processes influence a person's ideas *directly*, but condition the state and position of his body *indirectly*, i.e., through the medium of processes at other and lower levels; nobody can merely "think" himself into motion – or, more precisely, the mere idea of locomotion is not of itself sufficient to cause locomotion. It would appear, then, that all – or practically all – human behaviour is determined, both directly and indirectly, by the processes of a number of structural levels of activity which – because of the fact that the lower levels are subsumed, or involved, in the more complex structures of the higher levels – can act through the medium of each other.

However, these structural levels of activity – physical, chemical, biological, psychological, ideological – which mutually interact *within* the human organism and so determine it from within, manifest themselves also in the universal environment of that organism, and so determine it from without. Thus, the ideological influence of one person upon another – necessitating, as it does, the communication of ideas – involves the activity of processes which are ideological, psychological, biological, chemical and physical; and moreover, the structure of process – levels involved in the communication of ideas, is duplicated for each individual concerned: one set existing internally for each organism, and another, existing externally to it.

The complete process of idea communication, in its complex transformations of energy from higher to lower levels, and back again from lower to higher levels, is very crudely analogous to the movement of a person from the top storey of a building through several floors to ground-level, along this level to the ground-floor of another building, and so up, once again, to the top storey. So far as the lowest level is concerned there is no qualitative distinction between the ground-floor level of the buildings themselves and the level of the area which separates them; *at this level, therefore, there is no sharp distinction between the buildings and their environment*; but, as a consequence of the storey-structure of the buildings, the top floors of different buildings possess a certain independence, both of each other and of the ground-level from which they were raised.

Normally, all the information about other attic-dwellers, which comes to the occupants of the top floor of each building, must come *via* the other floors and ground-level. Therefore, the observational facts – with which all science must systematically begin and which form, so to speak, its raw material – are, for the study of ideological structure and development, to be found in the means by which people communicate with each other.

2.3 Cognitive Assumptions

IT will be obvious that the clarity of our conception of an ideology will largely depend upon the clarity of our conception of the leading terms we employ in its definition and description. We have said that cognitive assumptions and affective identifications are, respectively, the bricks and mortar of which an ideology is composed. Let us examine these materials more closely. Firstly, what do we mean by "cognitive assumptions"?

The word "assume," according to the dictionary, means to "take upon oneself" or to "take for granted." "To grant" is to bestow, to allow, to concede, to admit, to accept as right, valid, correct, legitimate or true; "to accept" is to consent to receive. A little consideration of these terms will show that there are involved in them two intimately related and fundamental ideas: (1) the idea of "taking" – of separation or distinguishing – and (2) the idea of "giving" – of associating or identification. These two fundamental ideas necessarily involve and mutually interpenetrate each other. Every act of "taking" or separation is also, at the same time, an act of "giving" or association. For example, the act of *giving* consent is at once the same thing as *taking or accepting* a request; my taking possession of an article is precisely the act of my giving it an owner; if I give something away then I take leave of it; taking a person indoors is the same as giving him entrance. Similarly, every act of separation is, at one and the same time, the act of uniting or joining: for a thing which is being separated from another is also that which is joining the group or class of separated things – which group, or class, also includes (precisely to the extent to which the process of separation is carried through) just that from which the thing is being separated; the two joined things *both* become two separated things.

Again, every act of distinguishing is precisely the act of associating or identifying: for when we distinguish something from something else we can only do so in so far as we associate it with distinguished things – including, of course, that from which the thing has become distinguished; conversely, when we associate something with some other thing we can only do so in so far as we distinguish it from distinguished things including, of course, that other thing with which it is being associated: for the more a thing becomes identified with another the less it is being an "other" itself – it is therefore becoming more distinguished from the other. The dialectic principle involved here is of the highest importance for the more adequate comprehension of ideological states and processes – for it applies to all antithetical, opposing and conflicting conditions – but we cannot now enter further into the matter and must leave it for fuller treatment elsewhere.

An assumption, then, is something which is "taken upon oneself," or "taken for granted," or "taken as conceded," or "taken as accepted," or "taken as admitted," or "taken as given." Evidently, whatever it may be which is assumed – whether it be a rule, an office, a disguise, an aspect, a function, a posture, a right, a principle, a truth or a fact – it is something which is *taken*. But equally, according to the principle we have just discussed, it should be something which is just as much *given* – and we shall find it is so. That is to say; an assumption is something in one's experience which is given the character or status of "reality" – of being a self, *like one's own self*; of having, in other words, a separate or independent identity of its own, *like one's own identity.* Thus, the act of assuming is the act of associating, or identifying, with oneself, something which is, at the same time, *distinguished* from oneself. To put it another way, that which is assumed is given the character of independent or real existence. When we realise that all our beliefs, knowledge, understanding etc. are concerned with what is independently real or true and what is not independently real or true, then we shall clearly see how intimately the process of assumption is involved in them.

It may be objected that the act of assumption involves the acceptance of something as real or true, *but without warrant or proof.* While the word is commonly used in this sense we cannot *wholly* admit this objection, since particular proofs are a relative matter. There is no particular proof which is absolute for all; and, whatever proof there may be forthcoming for the truth or reality of something, it may convince one but not another. We are all prepared to accept some things on the slightest of evidence; on other matters we require more pressure of evidence. Every act of assumption takes place as the result of a certain amount of compulsion or force, however little; so that, whatever the stage at which we may succumb to the pressure of evidence for something, whether it be when the weight of evidence is of the slightest amount, or when it is massive and of the greatest amount, in every case we are *forced* to make the assumption. Therefore whenever, in common parlance, we use the word assumption to mean "acceptance without proof," what we really mean is "acceptance with relatively little proof." Even the mere conceivability of something constitutes *some* evidence of its independent existence, if only as an independent or distinct idea within the mind.

We repeat, then, that an assumption is something in one's experience which, *under some sort of compulsion or force,* however great or small, is given the character of independent or real existence, is given the status of reality, or an identity of its own similar to one's own identity. The process involves, at one and the same time something *taken* and something *given.* We can now more easily see that what is taken, accepted or received is really the compulsion, the limiting pressure or force exercised by that which is being assumed; in other words, when one makes an assumption one takes or accepts a *limitation* upon oneself. And we can now see that what is *given,* given up, or handed over, as it were, is one's own independence of the limitation: the limitation is itself given a measure of independence, i.e. is "given" real existence. A kind of exchange takes place, and we propose to borrow two convenient terms from psychoanalysis to describe the two mutually interpenetrating aspects of this exchange; they are *"introjection"* and *"projection,"* and we shall regard them as antithetical aspects of one and the same process – a process which, in its more complex forms at least, constitutes a special kind of reaction of the individual organism with its environment. With these terms we can now describe the act or process of assumption as involving (a) the introjection of a limitation or determining influence of some kind, and (b) the projection of independence or, what amounts to the same thing, the projection of self-dependence or self-determinism.

It is of interest, in this connection, to reproduce the following remarks from McDougall's *Frontiers of Psychology.* He says (pp. 108-9):

> ... Ultimately, belief in reality of any and every kind rests upon
> and, directly or indirectly, is induced only by, resistance to our
> effort, to our own striving. That which can resist us physically or

otherwise, can act upon us compulsively, is the real, is believed in. Such experiences are the common root or ground of our belief in the reality of things; and not only of physical things, but of all that we regard as real... All belief in real things has, then, this two-fold root; first, one's experience of one's self as enduringly the same being, powerful in the sense that, though not always active, it is always capable of activity, of putting forth power. Secondly, one's experience of things (primarily persons and animals) which similarly endure and manifest to us their power by acting upon us, resisting or compelling us. In this foundation of all belief in real things we see the deepest root of primitive animism. For to primitive man, as to the child, persons are the most compelling and therefore the most real as well as the most interesting of objects; animals come near them and are conceived after the model of the person; while the inanimate thing is similarly patterned after the person, the model of all reality, and is only gradually deprived of all attributes of persons, except in space and time, and power.

Now, we shall find that the process of assumption is a necessary condition for the existence of intentional or voluntary behaviour. As we pass in review the whole evolutionary scale of organic life we find that living things behave, not merely according to the laws which govern inanimate matter, but also spontaneously, partly of themselves, according to other laws; and the higher we ascend in this scale the more do we find that living things seem to behave with purpose and design, to anticipate and expect events, until, when we arrive at the culminating point of man himself, we find him acting more with deliberation, intent and foresight than any other animal. Of all living creatures the human being is the most capable of spontaneous adjustment of his behaviour to the reality of environmental conditions. This adjustment of behaviour involves a high degree of understanding and knowledge, and these in turn involve the process of assumption. For, to act with intent and purpose, it is necessary to base such action on something in one's experience which is "given" the character of independent reality or existence; it is necessary to assume something or other – something must be taken for granted. Without assumption there is, and can be, no purpose, no intention, no design, no foresight, no intelligence or intellect, no knowledge or understanding.

Assumptions, therefore, because they are the necessary conditions of all intentional behaviour, are implicit in all expressions of meaning, purpose, design and intelligent action; they underlie, as implications, all statements of fact, expressions of opinion, belief and understanding. And, as it is the occupation of science to discover the particular conditions necessary for the existence of particular phenomena, it is therefore the business of science to study the process of assumption and to systematise the relations between different kinds or structures of assumption and different kinds of behaviour.

If I say to a friend "Lend me five pounds!" then that is an action, a piece of behaviour. We can explain the action in its details in terms of mechanical, physical, chemical, biological processes and laws, and no doubt show other instances of these latter operating in other fields and classes of phenomena; yet, but for the process of assumption and the whole complicated structure of assumptions upon which that statement is made, *the action with all its details could never occur at all.*

Apart from the intent or meaning of the particular words I use, the mere action of speaking to my friend involves a large number of assumptions; it implies, for example, that he is a conscious being, that he understands the English language, that he is not deaf, that he is paying attention to what I am saying and so on. But for these assumptions, made on my part, I should not speak at all. The particular request itself contains and exhibits a whole host of assumptions: it implies that my friend has five pounds to lend; it takes for granted that he is the kind of person who would lend that sum; it presupposes that I need five pounds; it assumes that the terse form of my demand will not cause him to be offended so that he will be likely to refuse; it takes for granted that I am a sane and rational individual; and so on and so on. But for these assumptions I should never make my request; and but for certain assumptions and the process of assumption itself, I *could* not do so.

Some of these assumptions will be found to underlie other actions and statements of mine. Some of them, indeed, will be implied by all or nearly all my intentional activity, and these will obviously be the most important from the point of view of ideological study; for they will constitute the more permanent and fundamental parts of an individual's ideological structure. Again, some of these assumptions will be found only from time to time in the behaviour of other people, but some of the more enduring and fundamental of them will be found to correspond with the more permanent and fundamental structures of others. It will thus be possible, on this basis, to group people together as belonging to one ideological class or another.

When we come to examine some of the different assumptions involved in some statement or action, we shall find that some are more "immediate" and explicit – e.g. in the above case: that I need five pounds – while others appear more "remote" and more deeply implicit – e.g. that I am a rational being. On the whole, the difference corresponds broadly with the distinction we have just made between the less permanent and the more permanent parts of ideological structure: for when we change our intentions or the meaning of our utterances – as we are constantly doing – what we really change are the more immediate and explicit of our assumptions; the more remote and implicit assumptions remain. Thus, throughout the continual changes of our meaning or intentions the more basic and underlying parts of them remain unchanged. We do not, therefore, ever alter *entirely* and *absolutely* our intentions; our meaning is never *wholly* and *completely* changed; it is merely modified and is continually undergoing modification. Apart from these continual and most superficial of modifications in our intentions as we go about our many and various daily tasks – changes which correspond with the continual changes in our movements, our behaviour and attitude – there do occur, of course, from time to time, deeper modifications in our ideological structures. These modifications, however, of the more permanent assumptions are much slower and – although they affect a wider range of our behaviour than do the changes of our more immediate assumptions – manifest themselves only after comparatively long intervals of time. Such deeper changes, as might be expected, are themselves more enduring and permanent than those superficial changes which are continually occurring. Yet, profound as these slower modifications may be, the fact still remains that there are even more fundamental assumptions which are left relatively unchanged. As we shall later see, the most fundamental of all assumptions remains throughout life.

We have provisionally and tentatively defined an assumption as an aspect or part of one's experience which, under some kind of compulsion or force, is given the character of independent existence or "reality." But this, of course, does not mean that all assumptions are necessarily true. In the case, given above, of my request for five pounds, I may not have noticed that my friend was asleep. Yet my action in asking for five pounds assumes that he is awake. Successful action would seem, then, to depend upon having the right assumptions – i.e. true assumptions. And, equally, the truth of an assumption will depend upon whether the action which is based on it, or in which it is implicated, is successful or not. This criterion of the truth of assumptions, however, is not quite so simple as it appears at first sight; for as we have seen, every definite aim or intention which issues in action, every definite meaning which finds utterance is really a whole complex of aims or meanings, more or less definite according to the nature of the assumptions upon which they are based. In short, aims, objects, intentions, meanings etc. are relative to the assumptions upon which they are founded, i.e. some are more immediate, superficial and changing, and others are more remote, permanent and fundamental. Not all successful action or behaviour, then, can be seen in a glance, or at once; the truth of some assumptions – the less immediate or more permanent and fundamental assumptions – can thus only be "tested" over a period of time, and this probably accounts, in part at least, for the comparative slowness in their modification.

This brings us to the question of how assumptions come to change and to undergo modification. As we have seen, our more immediate aims and intentions, objects and meanings, are continually changing through-out our everyday waking lives. What causes them so to change? We have also noted the slower and more ponderous changes of our more ultimate aims and intentions. One cause of change, of both the more immediate and the more fundamental assumptions, we have just been discussing: unsuccessful action. The lack of success in achieving one's aims – frustration – is a common experience of all; and it is this frustration – experience which forces us to modify our assumptions. How this occurs in detail is a matter for further treatment and fuller examination.

There is, however, another cause of change in our aims and purposes which we must clearly observe. It is that formed by the constantly changing nature of our environment, the changes of stimuli to which all organisms are continually subject. Some of these changes are brought about by one's own intentional activity, and some by the intentional activity of others. But this introduces us to a complication; here, again, things are no quite so, simple as they at first appear. For, not only are we subject to changes of stimuli caused by mechanical, physical, chemical and biological changes, in our external environment and in our own bodies – our "internal" environment – but in addition, we are subject to changes of stimuli caused by our own intentional behavior and the aims intentions and meanings of others. In other words besides that part of our environment which we can see hear, touch, smell etc., there is another part which is psychological and ideological; it is a part of our environment which, though unseen and manifested to us through the medium of mechanical, physical, chemical and biological processes – we are nevertheless forced to recognise as just as real.

We have already drawn attention, in the last chapter but one, to this particular aspect of our environment. But the matter is more complicated. Just as there are mechanical, physical, chemical and biological processes going on internally as well as externally, so, similarly, with psychological and ideological processes. And this *internal* psycho-ideological environment constitutes the most immediate part of our whole universal environment. Moreover, sensations of stimuli from the world outside our bodies and from our bodies themselves – stimuli that have their origin in mechanical, physical, chemical, ideological, psychological and ideological processes – of which we become aware, are all given meanings of some kind or another; that is to say, they become associated with or assimilated into, the whole system or structure of our cognitive assumptions, and by thus giving them meaning and reality they become transformed into assumptions themselves. As I pause from writing, for instance, I hear noises of what I *assume* to be the footsteps of people walking in the street below, the barking of a dog in the distance, the ringing of a telephone bell in the house next-door, the dustman dropping an empty dustbin on the hard pavement outside, and so on. Unless I make these, or some similar, assumptions the world outside remains a mere meaningless jumble of noises.

Again, I hear sounds which I *assume* to be those of two people approaching and engaging in loud conversation. At first, I cannot hear distinctly the actual words of their discussion, though I *assume* from their manner that they are both rather angry. As they pass under my window – or more accurately, as I assume them to be passing under my window – I catch some of the words I *assume* they are uttering. A new element now enters the situation: I not only regard myself as perceiving that two people are passing under my window engaged in loud and angry conversation, *but I also regard myself as perceiving the meaning of some of the words they utter.* The new element consists, in short, in the fact – or, what amounts to the same, in the assumption – that I "know" *what* they are saying in addition to "knowing" that they are saying something. To put it another way: *that* which they are saying, or expressing, is their meaning or intention – that is to say, they are expressing the ever-changing structures of their cognitive assumptions – and in the same way that I give reality (or independent existence) and meaning to the sounds of footsteps, voices, etc. (by making assumptions and assimilating them into my own ideological structure of cognitive assumptions) so similarly do I give reality and meaning to *that* which they are saying. I come to "know" something of "what is passing in their minds," to know some of their "passing thoughts " – i.e. I come to know some of their more immediate and temporary assumptions.

This leads us to touch briefly upon the problem of agreement and disagreement. In the case of the two people referred to above, it was assumed that they were "in disagreement with each other." It is often said of two such persons that they cannot "see each other's point of view." A statement of this kind is an approximation to our newer conception that – whether the disagreement revolves around questions of fact or principle, or whether it involves questions of "ought" or "ought not " – such people differ largely because neither can assimilate the other's immediate or explicit assumptions into his own ideological structure in the same way as does the other. (We say "largely" because we have yet to deal with the very important affective or emotional aspect which although not exclusive of the cognitive aspect, is expressed more in the *manner* of utterance and behaviour.) Differences of opinion may be superficial, involving more or less broad differences between the more immediate and temporary assumptions of people; or they may be more deep-seated, involving differences between the more permanent assumptions – as in disputes between two people of different ideological groups. We have already observed in the last chapter that in the same way no two persons possess *exactly* the same physiological structure, though alike both broadly and in many details, no two persons will have exactly the same ideological structure; any two people, therefore, will always be able to find something about which they disagree, even though they may find agreement upon what are frequently called "broader issues," i.e. the more permanent assumptions. However, we cannot properly and adequately treat this topic of agreement and disagreement among people without first coming to some understanding of emotional identification, which we must leave for subsequent pages.

Before passing on to the next chapter, there is another point that is worth mentioning here, which is closely allied to the problem of conflicting assumptions and disagreement between different people. It is: that we shall find the phenomenon of conflicting assumptions and disagreement in *the ideology of one and the same person* to be a normal and universal characteristic of ideologies. We shall learn, moreover, (a) that these internal conflicts within an ideology are concerned, not only with the more temporary assumptions, but also with the more permanent and fundamental parts of the ideological structure; (b) that in order to prevent these internal conflicts from interfering with the intentional behaviour and utterances of the individual, whole groups or layers of assumptions are kept from expressing themselves in the normal way – viz. through the conscious aims, intentions and meanings of a person – by a process of repression or inhibition; and (c) that these internal conflicts are intimately bound up with and partly determine the external conflicts between different persons and different ideological groups of people.

Though we have hardly skimmed the surface of the whole subject of cognitive assumptions, enough has been said, I feel, to show that any attempt to explain the whole of human behaviour solely in mechanical, physical, chemical, biological and psychological terms still leaves a good deal of human behaviour unexplained and not understood – as witness, e.g., the universal bewilderment and impotence in face of the increasing problems of ideological conflict within society. This important lacuna in our understanding, the present writer suggests, can largely be filled in only by the development of an independent science and study of ideology; a science which must first begin, at least, with the study of the ideology of the individual, the unit of the group; a science which is as distinct from psychology as psychology is from biology, and biology from chemistry, and chemistry from physics – and, of course, just as much connected with these sciences as these are with each other. For we shall hold that, just as we find biological processes, when analysed and broken up into their detailed constituent processes, become merely a group of separate, isolated chemical, physical and mechanical processes; and, just as we find that when we do the same with chemical processes, their isolated constituents become merely physical and mechanical; and similarly when we break up physical processes into the mechanics or dynamics of material particles or wave systems; so in the same fashion, when we come to analyse ideological processes into their structural constituents, we shall find them in proportion as the breaking-up procedure of analysis is carried far – to be psychological, biological, chemical, physical, and mechanical.

This procedure of breaking up the directly unobservable into the directly observable – that is, into more and more isolated units of a more directly observable nature – has its limits. For, when the analytic procedure is continued beyond these limits, the directly observable merges once more into the directly unobservable. But it must not be taken, that, because a thing is not directly observable – i.e.

is observable only indirectly – it therefore has no independent being. Though the indirectly observable may have a different mode of existence from the more familiar and observable, that it *has*, indeed, an independent being – with laws, processes, and a structure of its own – is attested by the time-honoured criterion of truth, including scientific truth itself, namely: that action based on ignorance of its nature, or indifference to its laws, leads eventually and inevitably, sooner or later, to frustration. Even those who may verbally deny the independent reality of the ideological realm are *forced to act in other ways* as if they conceded, at least, just that; while denying its *de jure* existence, they must perforce accept it *de facto*.

Although external stimuli play a great part in the determination of human behaviour, man's actions cannot be *wholly* explained in mere terms of mechanical, physical, chemical, biological or psychological reactions to external stimuli, for these reactions are also modified, conditioned and determined by a complex ideological system of cognitive assumptions. By chopping up (an intentional procedure which is itself largely determined by an ideological structure of assumptions), by breaking up human behaviour into sufficiently detailed, isolated, and observable component actions, we find we can explain each of them in biological, chemical, physical, or mechanical terms – according to the extent to which the breaking-up procedure is carried – without ever being compelled to assume the objectivity (or independent reality) of ideological processes; as external, objectively real processes, they simply do not enter the matter, for they have been *effectively excluded by the analytical procedure of breaking up and destroying the connected nature of the actions – and it is with the connection, the correlation and integration of such mechanical, chemical, physical, biological and psychological activities, that ideological processes are concerned.*

Without this connected nature, without the correlation and integration (without, in word, the modification or *control*) of multitudinous separate activities and reactions to stimuli involved in doing something, saying something, thinking something, or going somewhere, without this connected nature, there could be no intentional behaviour of any kind – including, of course, the procedure of analysis, of breaking up this connected nature, and of explaining the separate actions in terms which entirely ignore their ideological context. Providing the breaking-up procedure is carried far enough, we could, in the same way, by a series of successive stages, firstly exclude or eliminate the psychological connections and interrelations of the separate activities, then, as the activities became more and more chopped up, sever them from their biological connections and interrelations, their chemical connections, then the physical, until we are left with the dynamics or movements – the activities – of infinitesimally minute and relatively unknown entities which turn out to be structures or systems of "waves."

Further steps in the breaking-up procedure lead us more and more to the point where it becomes obvious: (1) that the analytic process cannot go on *ad infinitum*, it comes to an end; (2) that the more we break up our activity into simpler and simpler elements, the less distinction we are able to make between the activities themselves and that which acts, until – as is practically the case with the "wave" – the distinction is entirely lost; (3) that the end-product of the analytic process must necessarily be a simple, structureless activity, incapable of further breaking up, and which, because of the fact that it has been severed from *all* its connections and interrelations, is therefore an entirely unmodified, unconditioned, and completely indetermined and indetermining activity – a mere featureless being that, because of its absolute isolation, is quite unobservable, directly or indirectly, and which, therefore, is just as much a non-activity, a non-existence: in fact, it must be nothing at all[1]. By separating the activities from all their particular connections, their special interrelations with each other, by isolating them *absolutely* – i.e. by annihilating *all* their *separate and distinguishable* connections – we destroy also *their separation and isolation from one another*, for we destroy all the special ways in which they are distinguished from each other as *distinct* and *particular* entities. Without definite positions or locations, without particular attributes or qualities, without definite size or magnitude these finite activities at last become an infinity of indistinguishables; they become an indefinite mass, a completely undifferentiated homogeneity. They thus lose their separate identities and merge into a completely and purely *general* connection with each other: that of merely *being* – unconditioned, unrelated, unqualified, indetermined and entirely independent – no longer being things or activities but just nothing, or space.

We see, then, that we cannot adequately explain human behaviour simply and solely by separating it up into independent, observable and isolated reactions to external stimuli. For, by tearing these reactions out of their ideological context, by sundering the connections between them, through which alone they are integrated into sequences of purposive and intentional behaviour, we destroy the very conditions under which ideological phenomena become possible; we abolish the very interrelations through which the ideological processes manifest themselves, and through which the various reactions are modified, conditioned, and determined by the ideological system of cognitive assumptions. The analytic procedure is indeed necessary and essential; we cannot get along without it. But it must be realised that the end-products of analysis are but a *part of the whole analytic process*, and derive what significance they have only from their *relations* to all the preceding stages of the material being analysed, including the original unanalysed condition of the initial raw material with which the analysis started. This integration and relation of the products of the analysis throughout *all* its stages – the raw material, the intermediate products and the end-products – this process of correlation and connecting up of all the threads undone by analysis, is the process of synthesis, and must be realised as a necessary and integral part of the complete analytic procedure. As we have mentioned above, the whole procedure of analysis is itself an intentional activity, and any part of the process can, therefore, only have any meaning or significance in its connections and relations to every other part of the process.

---

[1] See Eddington's *The Philosophy of Science.*

2.4 The Proccess of Assumptions

WE are now in the position where we understand: (a) that all our beliefs, opinions, knowledge, understanding etc. are concerned with what is "real" – or has independent being – and what is not real; (b) that the "attribute" or "quality" of reality – or independent being – is always conferred by the process of assumption; (c) that the act or process of assumption is a reciprocal activity of introjection and projection, and is a specific reaction – objective as well as subjective – of the individual organism; (d) that the process of assumption occurs at the instance of some kind of determining influence or force – that is to say, it is a process which is determined mechanically, physically, chemically, biologically, psychologically and *ideologically*; (e) that every idea has meaning – or, in other words, is an idea – in so far as it results from the association, relation or interaction of a particular stimulus (internal or external) with a structure of more or less general assumptions. Several questions now arise as to how assumptions are maintained, how they are related to each other and effect each other etc. But first, in order to gain clearer ideas of the nature of assumption, let us attempt to trace some connection or correlation between the assumptive process and the physiology of an individual organism.

The act of assumption, we have seen, is an ideological process. But in saying this, we do not mean that it is not also a psychological process; neither do we imply that it is not also a biological process; nor do we infer that it is a process which does not embody chemical, physical or mechanical activities. On the contrary, we must regard the ideological process as embracing within itself, and as dependent upon, all the other levels of activity – which levels exist also outside the ideological level, as largely independent process-levels, with each level embracing, in a similar fashion, processes of all the levels below it. Thus, the processes of the higher levels are more complex, heterogeneous and differentiated than those of the lower levels; for the processes of each level not only contain activities of all the lower levels, but contain them in such a way that, by their integration and connection with each other, they exhibit qualitatively new and different modes of activity – i.e. those modes of activity which are characteristic of the level. Only by such conceptions, for which there is a great deal of evidence and scientific warrant, is it possible to explain how, on the one hand, ideas can act upon and determine each other, and also, on the other hand, how ideas and matter can interact and mutually condition each other. Hence, according to this standpoint, ideas are real, active, capable of determining each other, and – per medium of the internal level – structure of ideological processes interacting with and through the subjacent external process-levels of determining organic and inorganic matter. Hence, too, material objects and organic bodies are capable of determining and conditioning ideas.

With these conceptions in mind, we can now approach the process of assumption from a point of view which takes into account its physiological nature or basis. We may, for instance, observe indirectly the process at work in the conditioning of the reflex activity of an individual organism. For the benefit of those who may not be familiar with reflexological nervous processes, we shall take the liberty of briefly describing such of them as are relevant and essential to our present discussion.

As the reader is doubtless aware, animal behaviour is now customarily divided into two types of response to external stimuli, both of which are reflex mechanisms. The first and more primitive type of reflex activity is inborn or inherited, and is exemplified in such actions as the sudden, automatic withdrawal of a person's hand when it is burnt or pricked. The mechanism is somewhat as follows: upon stimulation of a suitable local group of peripheral receptors or sense organs – which, because they are specifically sensitive to one particular mode of stimulation, peripherally select or analyse stimuli – trains of ingoing or afferent nervous impulses are set going along the nerve fibres of a number of sensory neurons which connect the peripheral receptors to the central nervous system, where the impulses are either wholly passed on to a number of motor neurons or relayed in part to the higher centres of the brain. By means of the nerve fibres of the motor neurons, the now outgoing or efferent impulses travel from the central nervous system to the effector organs – such as muscles or glands – which are thus excited into activity or inhibited from activity as the case may be. This is the mechanism of the unconditioned or absolute reflex, and is an innate or inherited nervous structure which functions without the active participation or intervention of the higher centres of nervous activity in the cerebral cortex of the brain. The withdrawal reflex, for example, is one of the functions of the spinal cord.

The second type of response is not quite so automatic and is more complicated than the first, though, as its name suggests, it is but a modification of the more primitive, inborn type of reflex. The mechanism of the conditioned or acquired reflex, as investigated by Ivan Pavlov, the Russian physiologist, is broadly as follows: upon repetition of the situation in which the stimulation of any particular local group of peripheral receptors occurs within a limited period before the presentation of an unconditioned stimulus (the stimulus which evokes the inborn reflex) a nervous connection is established, *via* the sensory and motor areas of the cerebral cortex, between that group of receptors and the motor neurons which effect the inborn or unconditioned response. The newly established nervous connection is such that when the particular group of receptors is stimulated in the same manner as previously, whether or not it is followed by the presentation of the unconditioned stimulus, the response occurs as if it were brought about by the unconditioned stimulus, and is, from external observation, in every way similar to the unconditioned or absolute response itself.

Thus the repetition of the situation wherein the sight of food is soon followed by the eating of it (a situation which obviously is constantly occurring among animals) establishes within the individual a nervous connection between the receptors of the retina and the motor neurons which control the salivary glands; so that, when the individual sees food, impulses from the retina of the eye are conveyed to the visual area of the cerebral cortex, and subsequently to the motor area of the cortex; the cortex passes the impulses on to the motor neurons that excite the salivary glands into activity; and the mouth then waters. The appearance of the food has become a "signal" for eating, or rather, for the presence of food in the mouth. Before the establishment of this or some similar path of nervous activity, the mouth waters only on presentation of the unconditioned stimulus: i.e. the presence of food in the mouth. On presentation of this latter stimulus, the nervous impulses travel along an inborn nerve path from the taste organs or receptors of the tongue, to a lower centre of the brain where are situated the motor neurons which pass on the impulses, by means of their nerve fibres, to the salivary glands. This is the unconditioned type of reflex which, in every case, forms the foundation for the establishment of the more complicated conditioned reflex.

Once a conditioned reflex is established, in order to maintain it, it becomes necessary from time to time to "reinforce" the conditioned stimulus with the unconditioned or absolute stimulus. For if the conditioned stimulus is not reinforced, if it is repeatedly received without being followed by the absolute stimulus, it gradually becomes "extinguished." That is to say, instead of it continuing to evoke the response with the same intensity as before, each time it is repeated its efficacy diminishes until finally there is no response at all. What happens is not the gradual obliteration of the acquired nervous connections, but the gradual establishment of new paths which increasingly have the effect of actually inhibiting the excitatory action of the conditioned stimulus, until, when the new inhibitory paths are fully established, the inhibition is more or less complete. This state of "extinction" of a conditioned reflex can itself be inhibited or extinguished. It happens when, in the early stages of extinction, as the conditioned response is growing more feeble, the conditioned stimulus is reinforced again by the unconditioned stimulus. The growing inhibition is inhibited, and the response now reappears with its previous intensity, which, however, again gradually diminishes if the conditioned stimulus continues to be presented without reinforcement.

Inhibition can occur in other ways. If, for example, during the presentation of a conditioned stimulus, a strange new stimulus of sufficient strength is simultaneously presented, the conditioned response will not occur; it will be inhibited. Similarly, if during the process of extinction of a conditioned reflex a strange stimulus of sufficient strength is presented, the disturbance will inhibit the inhibitory extinction and the conditioned reflex will return with some, or all, of its former intensity. Again, inhibition occurs in the process of "discrimination," which we can briefly describe as follows.

Suppose a particular sound – say, of a gong – be established as a conditioned stimulus for the salivary response of a dog. At first the stimulus will be more or, less "generalised" – that is to say, the response will occur for a given range of sounds which are similar to, but not the same as, the original sound. If, however, the different sounds are presented one after another at fairly frequent intervals, but the unconditioned stimulus – food – is given only after presentation of the original sound and not after any of the others, these other sounds cease, after a time, to evoke the response. The response to each of them has become extinguished or inhibited; only the response to the original sound remains. The animal has "learnt" the difference between the sounds; it "discriminates" between them.

In his experiments with dogs, Pavlov demonstrated the formation of chains of conditioned reflexes – that is to say, the establishment of a series of reflexes, built up one by one, each established upon the others already formed. This process produces an increasingly complicated and circuitous nerve path for the impulses to traverse before they can effect the response. Thus, where such chains of reflexes are established, the ingoing impulses are first passed to the sensory area of the cortex appropriate to the nature of the final conditioned stimulus, and thence, one after another, to the other sensory areas appropriate to the stimuli used in the previous stages of conditioning, and ultimately, to the motor areas of the cortex from which run the nerve fibres to the effector organs.

Now, it is obvious that these various physiological processes and, mechanisms concerning the conditioned reflex, involved in the higher mental activities of all human beings: for example, in learning the meaning of spoken words, in the growth of understanding, in the concentration and diffusion of attention, in the formation of aims, ideas, intentions and so forth. If the cerebral hemispheres of an animal brain are removed, its conditioned reflexes, and the modes of behaviour founded, upon them, are absent or destroyed; only its automatic, inborn reflex activity remains. Such an animal – a decerebrate dog, for instance – can breathe, swallow, walk, sleep and, if mildly hurt, snap and snarl; but it will only react to direct stimuli. It will starve, even though its usual food is within sight and within reach, unless meals are actually placed into its mouth. Though starving, it shows no sign of hunger – and all other signs of feeling or emotion are similarly absent. All those optical, olfactory, and auditory stimuli, which previously were capable of producing the most violent reactions, now become meaningless for the animal and quite ineffective. Such a decerebrate animal lacks the ability to learn, to remember, to understand, to anticipate, or to interpret any kind of signal – in short, it is largely *non est* mentally.

Thus, from the physiological point of view, the mechanism of the conditioned reflex plays a great and essential part in the growth and nature of understanding, and consequently in all "drive" or intentional behaviour. Yet we have seen that, from the ideological view-point, the process of assumption is also a necessary and essential foundation for all understanding and intentional activity. If this is the case, though it would be an obvious error to attempt to identify the conditioned reflex with the process of assumption, it is nevertheless forced upon us to conclude that the assumptive process is necessarily involved in the establishment and operation of the conditioned reflex. When Pavlov's dogs respond to the conditioned stimulus with "signs of appetite" that is to say, with activity of the salivary and gastric glands, and of the muscles involved in lip-licking, champing of the jaws, barking, tail-wagging and other motor reactions – it is difficult to avoid the conclusion that the animals "expect" the appearance of food, that they "*assume*," in some simple primitive way, that they are about to eat. It should be noted that we gain this unavoidable impression largely because of the connected and related nature of these different reactions. Barking alone, or mere tail-wagging, or champing of the jaws only, or even the activity of salivating unaccompanied by any of the other reactions – none of these events occurring alone and unconnected would so forcibly impress upon us the conclusion that these dogs were "anticipating" or showed signs of "expectation" and "foresight," and therefore were *assuming* the reality of something or other.

It should be noted also that we gain the above impression partly because we are unable to avoid reading or projecting our own subjective experience into the behaviour and experience of the dogs. This fact may, indeed, form the basis for strong objections to our procedure from certain people who regard it as an altogether and completely unwarrantable form of conducting inquiry. We shall not be deterred, however, and we need not let it worry us unduly; for, as we shall show explicitly – and we have already shown it to some extent – the procedure of projecting our subjective experience into things is a necessary and essential part of the process of understanding. So far from being completely and entirely illegitimate, no understanding or knowledge would be possible without it. It lies at the root, the beginning and foundation of our knowledge of matter; it is involved, as we have seen, in every act of assumption.

But this defense of our method must not be taken to mean that we are at liberty to read or project into objective things just what we like, or just such of our own subjective experience as we feel inclined. On the contrary, as we have already indicated, and as we shall later more clearly realise, projection always and under all circumstances occurs at the instance of some more or less compelling force, some compulsion or other – whether the projection be that of the savage or infantile mind in attributing emotions, thoughts, perceptions, sensations etc. to inanimate material objects, or whether it be that of the scientist in attributing to those same material objects the character or status of independent being or reality. For even the character of objectivity is *that* in our experience, is *that* aspect of our own subjective being – i.e. of being independently real – which we are compelled to project in order that the object becomes and remains intelligible to us. And, as we have pointed out above, the compulsion is not merely and exclusively ideological, but is psychological, biological, chemical, physical and mechanical as well. Thus we see, then, that although we need not be afraid of projection as such, we must be extremely careful to project only such as we are really forced or compelled to do in order that the phenomena become intelligible to us: we must not assume more than what, by the facts, we are *forced* to assume. This, of course, is simply another way of saying that we must not be compelled to make assumptions which arise from ignorance of available and ascertainable facts, and which, therefore, are avoidable. But assume we must, and project we must; we are compelled to do so if we are to have any kind of knowledge, or even the slightest degree of understanding. The person who utterly dismisses as completely and absolutely illegitimate the "reading of our own minds" or the "projection of subjective characteristics" into objective things, just doesn't understand the nature of his own knowledge and his own understanding of things. The very denial of the legitimacy of projection involves the projection of subjective characteristics into other people. This negative principle, or assumption, like so many others, cannot be acted upon or carried out with consistency because it is self-negating – for if carried out with complete consistency it leads to pure solipsism, to that very state of affairs from which it presumes, by implication, to rescue us.

In the particular case under discussion, therefore, we shall have no great qualms about attributing the process of assumption to the animal mind. As we have already remarked, if we take the facts in their connection and relation to each other and not as mere isolated and separate events, we shall be forced to the conclusion that the assumptive act is of necessity involved in the operation of the conditioned reflex. We are forced to the conclusion simply because, without it, the facts or actions, when fitted back into their contexts, remain unintelligible. Moreover, we shall find that our conclusion not only brings into close connection and harmonises two groups of facts which are drawn from two distinct but related spheres (the ideological and biological) and increases our present understanding, but also, that it is further confirmed by the later results and gains in our knowledge which accrue from its adoption. We shall, then, regard the animal-learning which is exhibited in the conditioning of reflex activity, as involving the process of making simple assumptions. The experimental dog – whose salivary reflex is conditioned to the stimulus of the flashing of an electric bulb or the sound of a buzzer or some other sensory experience – because it "recognises" the stimulus as a signal for eating pleasurable experience of overcoming the unpleasant feeling or painful internal stimulus of hunger) then "grasps" or "understands" in a simple primitive way, the "meaning" of the stimulus.

We have seen that the existence of an inborn reflex is a necessary condition for the establishment of a conditioned reflex, and that, therefore, the existence of an unconditioned stimulus is a necessary condition for the existence of a conditioned stimulus. Similarly, the presentation or reception of the conditioned stimulus becomes, temporarily at any rate, the necessary condition for the existence of the unconditioned stimulus – i.e. in the case of the salivary reflex, the presence of food in the mouth. Now, since an "implication" can be defined as "a necessary condition for the existence of some particular event, thing or other," we may alternatively assert that a particular conditioned stimulus *implies* a particular unconditioned stimulus; and that, within the limitations of the particular context in which it appears, the conditioned stimulus is *implied* by the unconditioned stimulus.

This mutual implication – this mutual relation of "necessary condition" – now enables us to regard the conditioned reflex as follows: upon reception of the conditioned stimulus, the animal "sees ," "perceives ," "grasps," "recognises" – that is to say, *assumes* – its implication, *viz.* the unconditioned stimulus (which, as we saw, besides producing the inborn response, causes impulses to pass up to the cerebral hemispheres). Or, in the case of chain-conditioning, where one stimulus implies several others, there are involved several corresponding acts of assumption. (We are reminded here of the fact that when we, ourselves, think of an event as a necessary condition for the existence of another event – i.e. as an implication of the latter – we think of the former as the "explanation" or "reason" for the latter. We form such chains as "I missed the opportunity because I was late," "I was late because I mistook the time," "I mistook the time because... " and so on and so forth.)

So far, in considering the conditioning process, we have tended to regard it as an establishment of new nerve paths and connections in the cerebral hemispheres, such that, when the conditioned stimulus is presented, impulses from the receptor organs simply travel up to the cortex through the new connections and down to the effector organs. But, of course, this is a very much distorted and over-simplified version of the real state of affairs. The element of memory – the retention of patterns of sensory experience – without which no conditioning or learning can occur, is left entirely out of the picture. In order to show its enormous importance let, us illustrate with an example.

Suppose the salivary reflex of a dog to be conditioned to an optical stimulus of some kind – the exposure, for a few moments, of a slowly moving white screen, say. The receptor-organs directly affected by the stimulus are the many millions of tightly-packed sense-cells of the retina of the eye – or rather, some of them. When the white screen is exposed, nervous impulses from these sense-cells are sent on their way up to the visual area of the cortex – where, it has been demonstrated, there is practically a point-to-point projection of the images falling upon the retina. Now then, it is obvious that during the exposure of the moving screen, the image on the retina will be in continual movement in relation to the retina itself, as will also the image's projection on the visual area of the cortex in relation to that area.

In other words, as the white screen moves, the actual sense cells engaged with initiating the nervous impulses directly relating to the screen, will be changing from moment to moment. And similarly with the neurons of the visual cortex, which are engaged with the reception of the impulses and their transmission to other parts of the brain. As the image shifts, some of the sense-cells and neurons directly affected by it become engaged with impulses concerning images of other, neutral stimuli; and on the other hand, some of the sense-cells and neurons engaged with these latter stimuli become directly affected by the white screen. Wherever the image presents itself on the retina it makes no difference to the efficacy of the stimulus in evoking the response.

Impulses are continually streaming from all the millions of retinal sense-cells before, during and after the presentation of the stimulus. Yet the actual nerve connections in the brain which transmit these impulses – or some of them – into paths leading to the salivary effectors, come into operation only when the image of the moving screen falls upon the retina. From all this it becomes clear that the physiological mechanism of the conditioned reflex is not a mere coupling arrangement whereby a stimulus sets up impulses which automatically stream along fixed nerve paths into the nervous system, through it and out again, with their final manifestation in the response. It becomes even more obvious when we realise that the dog can be taught to discriminate between two white screens of different shape, so that the response occurs for one screen but not the other. Thus it is evident that what really matters is the *pattern* of sensory impulses, that it is the *pattern* of nervous activity received in the cortex which releases the impulses into the appropriate channels, and not the mere fact or presence of such activity. What is required to be fixed and un-changing is not so much the nerve paths and connections of the reflex mechanism, but the *main pattern of the sensory activity evoked by the stimulus* – and this involves retention and the process of assumption.

"Pattern," broadly speaking, is the arrangement or mutual relations, in space and time, of a number of unit-parts to form a whole, or group, which can be reproduced, repeated or *recognised* as such. Though it may not be so obvious as in the case of optical stimuli "pattern" is involved in the reception of every stimulus, whether it be the sound of a buzzer, the feel of velvet, the smell of new-mown hay, or the taste of vinegar. It is partly by its own characteristic or inherent pattern that we "recognise" a stimulus – that is to say, by the particular system of co-existences and sequences of nervous impulses, or units of nervous activity, which the stimulus evokes. What the ultimate objective units are, which we assume to form the basis of the innate pattern of the external stimulus, we cannot know through sensory channels – for to be thus known they must have a communicable pattern or structure, which would at once disqualify them from being ultimate unit-parts. But it doesn't in the least matter, for all we require is that the mutual relationships or arrangements – the co-existences and sequences between the unit-parts of the stimulus answer to, or correspond with, the pattern of the unit-parts of nervous activity.

We have already seen, above, how the conditioned-stimulus implies an unconditioned stimulus (or, in chain-conditioning, a series of stimuli) and how "recognition" depends upon the assumption of this implication – of this relation of "necessary condition." But we now see that recognition depends also upon the retention of the inherent pattern or mutual relations of the stimulus itself (of the unconditioned as well as the conditioned stimulus). Thus, in "recognition" we have two elements or aspects to consider: (1) the *internal* pattern of the stimulus and (2) the *external* pattern of stimuli – i.e. their mutual implication, their mutual relations with each other (forming patterns of sensory patterns). These two elements are closely bound up and dependent upon one another, and both – because they involve the formation and retention of "patterns," or mutual relations, upon which behaviour is founded – involve the process of assumption.

Unfortunately, very little is known of the actual physiological mechanisms and changes which underlie the retention of sensory patterns. There does seem some ground, however, for believing that retention of traces of sensation is accomplished by the relaying of sensory impulses to special groups of cyclically acting neurons, which continue to excite and re-excite one another after the particular stimulus responsible for the impulses has ceased to act upon the receptors.

Be that as it may, wherever we find the capacity to learn – and its most primitive forms are to be found very low in the animal scale of life – wherever, in other words, we find the capacity to form and retain new patterns of nervous activity, we must of necessity find the capacity, however primitive, to form assumptions. But, although the physiological basis for assumption is the establishment of a structure of nervous patterns, the process of assumption essentially consists in this: *the reception of these patterns as the patterns of an outer world*, and therefore, as determinants of, or limitations upon, behaviour. Hence, every act of assumption involves the relation between subject and object.

2.5 The Absolute Assumption

THE process of assumption, we have just seen, is intimately connected with the means by which a living organism maintains its relations with its environment, the external world. Those means are patterns of nervous activity. And patterns of nervous activity naturally require a nervous structure or system. Some patterns, or rather, some types of pattern, arise from a wholly inborn structure, and other types arise from a modification of this structure. Since the acquired types of pattern are based upon the inborn types, we may tentatively conclude that the most primitive and fundamental – as well as the most permanent – of our assumptions are inborn. And these, we might add, will be particularly manifested in all expressions of what we call instinct. Let us turn our attention for a moment in this direction.

As the nervous system has a phylogeny, or evolutionary history, so, we may infer, have the types of pattern representing the environment of the organism; and so too, therefore, have the appropriate types of assumption, and consequently, the process of assumption itself. The unit of the nervous system is the nerve-cell. These cells have developed, phylogenetically, by increasing specialisation and differentiation from a more generalised type, and ultimately of course, from a unicellular creature; a type so generalised in its functioning as to render it capable of independent existence, and of being, so to speak, its own nervous system. That a unicellular creature of this generalised nature can be such a one-celled "nervous system" is shown by the behaviour of the amoeba which, when a sharp beam of strong light is directed on to one part of it, reacts by contraction of the stimulated part and then by complete withdrawal from the beam. (Very strong light is injurious to the creature and may even kill it.) This simplest and least organised member of the protozoa is sensitive to certain other stimuli, all parts of its surface being equally sensitive; and impulses from a stimulated region actually travel throughout its whole body at a very slow but definite rate.

Here, in such an elementary creature as this, are the rudimentary, primeval beginnings of our own highly organised system of nervous activity, the complex patterns of which we identify with our internal and external environment. Though the primitive nervous activity of the unicellular protozoon can hardly be regarded in terms of "patterns," nevertheless, we cannot escape the fact that the rudimentary elements for nervous patterns are somehow present in the creature. And from these elements have developed, in the long course of evolutionary change, the types of nervous pattern which, we have seen, necessarily involve assumption, and along with which, therefore, has arisen the assumptive process, itself.

The assumptive process, then, is inborn and inherited as a necessary consequence of our inheritance of a ready-made system of nervous activity. It is a fundamental function of that activity – the function which prescribes that the patterns of the activity are those of independent existences, are those of a real world; the function which ensures that the patterns, or mutual relations of nervous activities, are identically those of "reality." Even those patterns we distinguish as mere flights of fancy, as the unreal products of imagination, we are compelled to assume as real products of a real nervous activity: in other words, we are compelled to regard them as *really* illusions and therefore, in some way, as part of reality.

Now, we have said that certain assumptions are more fundamental and permanent than others; we have also seen that some, at least, of these, are inborn. As assumptions are connected with the relation of nervous patterns to reality, then the more permanent and basic assumptions will be associated with those parts of the patterns which are the more enduring and constant features of patterns, and which are more common to them. On the other hand, the temporary and more superficial assumptions will be connected with those elements of patterns which are continually changing. The most fundamental element of all of these patterns will obviously be that which has persisted in all types of pattern throughout evolutionary history, and which has come down to us from the very earliest times, from the very beginnings of primeval nervous activity. It is, we suggest, with this fundamental component of our patterns that our most fundamental and permanent assumption is bound up. And, for the very reason that it is the most elementary and permanent of all assumptions, it is the most likely, in our normal, everyday intercourse with our environment, to escape notice. Let us attempt to isolate this assumption (the one to which all others must be assimilated) and endeavour to discover how it manifests itself in our behaviour.

In an earlier chapter, when trying to come to grips with the nature of assumption, we asserted that the process involved something taken and something given. It involved introjection and projection. We then added that what was introjected, or received, was a limitation of some sort, and what was projected, or given up, was one's independence of the limitation. It will now be readily seen that all stimuli constitute limitations – which is, of course, another way of saying that all stimuli condition. The limitation, then, which is introjected in the process of assumption, is a stimulus of some kind. (We have already learned that an assumption takes place under some kind of compulsion.) However, we can no longer confine the idea of a stimulus to mean a simple sensory pattern. We have seen that such a stimulus has an inherent pattern which we have called "sensory." But we also came to understand that there are other nervous patterns which are patterns or mutual relations of sensory stimuli – in other words, patterns of sensory patterns. These patterns of patterns we shall now include under the term stimuli. And in order to distinguish them from mere sensory patterns – from the patterns or stimuli which are directly sensated – in order to distinguish those that form mutual relations *between* sensory patterns, we shall use the term "abstract stimuli." This enables us, when we assert that the introjected limitation is a stimulus of some sort, to include in the assertion those assumptions which are ideologically determined – i.e. those assumptions which are formed when certain ideas influence us.

Introjection, we see then, is necessarily the introjection of a stimulus, *sensory* or *abstract*. The other aspect of the assumptive process – projection – involves, as we have said, something given; and we can now readily understand that what is given is a *reaction* of some kind. In the case of a simple sensory stimulus the reaction begins with the effect of the stimulus upon the receptors or sense-cells, which is then transferred to the processes or fibres of other cells and so eventually to the brain, where the pattern of the stimulus is received and assimilated to either patterns (probably by reinforcement of the activity of numerous appropriate groups of cyclically connected neurons, which, it has been suggested, are bound up with memory or retention of pattern). The reaction then continues, *via* other cells, in the modification of one's behaviour – as, for example, in the operation or inhibition of some conditioned reflex or reflexes.

The whole reaction – which, in our own highly organised system, is a complex, or pattern, like the sensory stimulus itself – and each part of the reaction, thus entails the *expenditure* of energy. What, we venture to suggest, is actually given up in the process of assumption, what is actually projected – *is* a certain amount of energy. Further, we suggest that the total amount of energy involved in the projection, the total energy expended (for there will be some energy gained as well as lost) *is* equivalent to the loss of independence – i.e. the loss of freedom from the limitation of stimulus.

The case of the introjection of the abstract stimulus is basically similar in so far as it involves the giving of a reaction which necessitates the expenditure of energy. The abstract stimulus, we have seen, consists of relations between sensory stimuli; the presentation and introjection of the abstract stimulus depends, therefore, upon the more or less simultaneous introjection of its component sensory stimuli – either directly as in the conditioning process, or indirectly, as in the form of the presentation of written or spoken words (which, as intelligible propositions, each containing two terms and a copula, express relations between things). However, the whole reaction to the abstract stimulus, as might be expected, is more complex and subtle than the reactions to the mere sensory stimulus. For reasons of space we cannot deal in detail with it here. But enough has been said, at any rate, to show (a) that the process of assumption, when analysed into its constituents, reveals itself as a physical process as well as an ideological one, and (b) that the assumptive process is a unity which consists of the introjection of a stimulus (sensory or abstract always remembering the abstract stimulus includes the sensory) and the projection of a reaction.

Every stage in the introjection of the stimulus is at the same time, a stage in the projection of the reaction: each unit-cell taking part introjects a simple stimulus series of stimuli, and each cell projects a simple reaction or series of reactions. Let us return for a moment to the amoeba. Though much less specialised in its structure and functioning than the nerve-cell taking part in the complex assumptive process characteristic of highly organised systems of nervous activity, nevertheless, for this elementary unicellular creature the process is fundamentally and basically the same. It introjects a stimulus and it projects a reaction necessitating the expenditure of energy. When the amoeba withdraws or contracts that part of it subjected to the light-beam, it is reacting to a stimulus. But not only is it reacting; *it* is resisting a limitation. And when we examine the behaviour of organisms generally – throughout the whole scale of life from amoeba to man – we can see that it can be summed up in the one word: *resistance* – i.e. the escaping from or overcoming of limitations. All reactions, then, are resistances; and in this connection, such phrases as "struggle for existence" and "survival of the fittest" at once spring to mind. Again, it will be clear that all intentional behaviour, all our aims, objects and purposes, however many and various, have *as* a single common function, the overcoming of limitations: i.e. *resistance*.

If we can show that all organic behaviour, however simple or complex it may be, or whatever multitudinous forms it may take, is fundamentally and universally *resistance* to limitation, then, I venture to think, we shall be well on the way to the discovery of our fundamental assumption. But, although so far we have shown this in no little detail – from the simple behaviour of the protozoon to the complex sensory and ideological behaviour of human beings – we have to remind ourselves of this important fact: namely, that organic creatures are also inorganic, and that the analysed details of all organic behaviour must, when severed from their organic connections, exhibit the behaviour of the inorganic – that is to say, must exhibit chemical, physical and mechanical behaviour. Can this, too, be encompassed by our generalisation? If so, if it can be so included, then down comes another barrier we have assumed to exist between the organic and the inorganic.

Now, it is a fundamental law of motion – and according to the scientific account, motion is omnipresent – as well as an axiom of physical science, that textitto every action there is an equal and opposite reaction. Every mechanical action is opposed by an equal reaction. Thus we are even compelled to think of a stationary object in terms of the resultant of two actions: one, of its downward movement toward the earth's centre of gravity, and the other, of its upward movement caused by the force exerted by that upon which it stands. This mutual resistance of action and reaction is universal. Every force is resisting and, at one and the same time, is being resisted by another; and every force is a limitation which is resisting the limitation of another such force.

Hence, we can now see that in all its main features: and all its details – inorganic as well as organic – the universally common and most fundamental function of the behaviour of living organisms is resistance to limitation. Action and reaction, stimulation and response, introjection and projection – these are, respectively, the physical, biological and ideological forms of the same basic process; a process which has evolved, from the beginning of time, to its final fruition in the assumptive process of the self-conscious mind.

All stimuli limit. Whether they be sensory or abstract stimuli, internal (from the body) or external, all stimuli constitute limitations. And all our complicated and involved behaviour consists in the interaction of forms of resistance corresponding to these various forms of limitation. But resistance ultimately implies the absence of limitation, i.e. it implies freedom and independence from limitation – it implies, in a word, self-determinism. We find we cannot even think of resistance to limitation without the thought of self-determinism: for if there is no self-determinism, if it be excluded from that which resists, then there can be no longer any resistance. Resistance exists in proportion as there is self-determinism, and resistance which is not self-determined, as well as determined, is meaningless and unintelligible. In all the physical reactions of matter, in all the biological responses of organisms, and in all ideological projections of the mind, there is resistance and therefore self-determinism.

Here, at last, we arrive at our fundamental, our most permanent and most primitive assumption, that into which all other assumptions must be assimilated, and that which constitutes the basis for the whole ideological structure of assumptions: it is the assumption that one is fundamentally self-determined (or indetermined, independent, unlimited, unconditioned or free). We shall see that the basic function of every form of resistance, every struggle, every wish or whim, every aim, every object or purpose, is to establish or confirm this assumption as far as is possible. Proteus-like, it manifests itself in all our activities. It underlies our instincts, our egoism, our love of power, of wealth, and even our love of knowledge.

Even when we willingly submit or subject ourselves to some limitation or other (as, of course, we are constantly doing) we do so only in so far as we think this subjection enables us to overcome a greater limitation. For instance, we willingly submit to the limitations imposed upon us in the getting of food in order to avoid the greater limitation imposed upon us by the internal stimulus of hunger. In fact, every successful action must be based on the acceptance of certain limitations (i.e. certain assumptions) which then become the means of overcoming the greater limitation otherwise suffered. This is how man becomes a more or less tamed or civilised animal. In accepting the limitations imposed upon him by relations with his fellows – in other words, by co-operating in social life – each member of the community avoids the greater limitations which he would otherwise have to suffer in isolation.

Again it is by acceptance of the limitations imposed upon him by intractable matter, that man is able to understand it and overcome those limitations. He subjects himself to its limitations in preparing the very techniques and contrivances which enable him to overcome its limitations and control matter. Science itself is essentially based on this submission to limitation in order to overcome limitation. Every person learns very early in life that, in approaching a brick wall with the intention of getting to the other side, it is necessary to submit to the limitations it imposes upon one's movements; it cannot be ignored.

Consider our so-called instincts. Internal stimuli in the form of physico-chemical events operating in conunction with inborn nervous structures, impose certain limitations upon us. In order to resist or escape the limitation and re-confirm the self-deterministic assumption, we are driven into certain forms of behaviour we call instinctive. However social life comes to modify instinctive behaviour, the fundamental assumption remains to express itself in all the modifications. The basic drive to political, economic and social struggle is in all cases the assumption of self-determinism – frequently voiced in such forms as "liberty," "freedom," "independence," "equality," or even "self-determination."

Thus, we see that the ultimate foundation for the whole ideological fabric of our assumptions is, paradoxically enough, the primitive inborn assumption that we are, ultimately, in our fundamental nature, unlimited, unconditioned, independent, indetermined and therefore free agents – in short, the assumption that, in our basic and final nature, we are absolute. We shall consequently refer to it as the "absolute" assumption (or, alternatively, the self-deterministic or indeterministic assumption).

Whether we know it or not we are all compelled to think in absolute terms. This fact is confirmed by a comparative study of ideologies. Even the ideologies which affirm that all things, or everything, is relative, must treat the "relative" as ultimate, fundamental, and absolute. (If *everything* is relative, then what is the whole class of relatives – the relative class – relative to? Since there can be nothing apart from *everything* then relativity can only be (a) relative to, or within, itself alone and (b) relative to nothing apart from itself. And this is just the nature of the absolute assumption.)

It is of interest and highly significant in connection with this innate fundamental assumption of self-determinism, to note that Pavlov's conditioned-reflex experiments forced him to conclude the existence of an innate "liberty" or "freedom" reflex in his dogs, and that, moreover, he was forced to conclude the instinct of "struggle" or "resistance" to be the most fundamental of instincts.

It is the absolute assumption which forms the basis of all our reality-conceptions. For when, in the process of assumption, we introject a limitation (in the form of a sensory or abstract stimulus) we react or "resist" that limitation, by "giving" it "reality" or independence – i.e. by the projection of self-determinism. And by so doing, by so giving the stimulus the fundamental character of our own identity, textitwe come to identify ourselves with the stimulus. As an assumption it becomes part of one's own being. We thus come to textitidentify ourselves with what we "know," or what amounts to the same, we textitidentify ourselves with the objects of our perception and understanding – that is to say, with that to which our perception and understanding refers. The whole question of "identification," however, requires separate treatment, and moreover is complicated by the process of inhibition or "repression." We shall proceed to deal with these two topics in the next chapters.

2.6 Identification

IDENTIFICATION, we have seen, is involved in the process of assumption and arises, fundamentally, from the projection of one's own independent identity, of one's own inborn assumption of independence or self-determinism. But, although identification first appears in the primitive assumptive process, and has its origin therefore in the absolute assumption, it soon begins to differentiate itself, in the ideological development, as a distinct activity with a certain amount of independence of the assumptive process, and a special function of its own. Let us consider, for a moment, how this happens.

Earlier on, in our discussion of the conditioned reflex mechanism, we mentioned the "signs of appetite," shown by the experimental dog when it was presented with an established conditioned stimulus. We also mentioned that a decerebrate dog gave no such signs of its feelings or emotions. It is evident from this that the cerebral hemispheres and the mechanism of the conditioned reflex play a great part in the existence and expression of emotions, particularly the higher and more complex emotions. How are we to interpret this display of feeling from the ideological viewpoint?

First of all, let us remember that, in the case of the experimental dog, the direct signs of appetite (e.g. watering of the mouth) are combined with obvious signs of pleasure (wagging of the tail and other motor reactions). Secondly, let us not forget that all these particular signs or reactions are dependent upon whether or not the animal is presented with certain internal stimuli representing the sensation of hunger. The animal that is replete with food will not give the usual response to the conditioned stimulus – in other words, the response will be inhibited.

All stimuli limit, we have said. But we have shown that not all stimuli limit equally and to the same degree, and that the overcoming of some limitations will take precedence over that of others, according to their relative intensity. Again, we have affirmed that all behaviour is resistance to limitation. But we have also shown that not all limitations will be resisted equally, and that the overcoming of some limitations will necessitate the inhibition of resistance to others. In the case of the hungry dog, the resistance to the internal limitation takes precedence over the resistance to the conditioned stimulus. But once this particular internal limitation is overcome and the animal is satiated with food, the resistance to the conditioned stimulus once more comes into operation. Other internal stimuli are now presented; the animal, replete with food, finds locomotion and other movements a burden. Energy which was available for the muscles of the limbs is now engaged with the activity of digestion. Resistance to this new internal limitation necessitates the inhibition of resistance to some other external conditioned stimulus – such, for example, as the sight of its kennel, to which the dog departs for rest, and the further overcoming of limitation.

Now, the overcoming of limitation, we saw, is the equivalent of the re-establishment or confirmation of the absolute assumption. This activity of overcoming limitation is also accompanied by the feeling of pleasure – which manifests itself in proportion to the intensity of the limiting stimulus that is being overcome. Thus, if the dog is very hungry it shows great pleasure at the sight of food; if less hungry then it shows correspondingly less pleasure; if not hungry it shows no sign of pleasure at all.

We have also seen, towards the end of the last chapter, that the reception of any sensory stimulus involves the incipient form of identification – as a consequence of the projection of its sensory reality or independent being. This applies also to all so-called neutral stimuli, that is to say, to all those stimuli which are resisted in the passive sense. In other words, besides the more or less generalised and partial inhibition of such stimuli, there exists in relation to them a generalised and incipient form of identification. In respect of these "neutral" stimuli, therefore, the nervous system is in a condition similar for that of muscles which are passive and "at rest." Such muscles are actually in a state of slight partial contraction or "*tone,*" as it is called. From our new viewpoint, therefore, the process of establishing the conditioned reflex consists of gradually inhibiting this initial partial or "tonic" resistance in respect of the particular stimulus which, among the numerous neutral stimuli, implies the unconditioned stimulus. And this inhibition of resistance occurs upon assumption of the implication.

The previous generalised and incipient form of the identification then becomes concentrated and particularised in the now conditioned stimulus; the new stimulus becomes, via the assumption, the outward and visible sign of the overcoming of limitation – i.e. *it becomes the necessary condition for the re-establishment of the absolute assumption.* On the other hand, the concentration and strengthening of identification in the conditioned stimulus has the effect of increasing the generalised inhibition of the remaining neutral stimuli. So that over a period of time (during which, an intense stimulus necessitating active resistance – such as the internal stimulus of hunger – is repeatedly overcome in association with a sensory pattern – of food – representing the conditioned stimulus) there is built up, on the one side, an increasingly strong identification with the conditioned stimulus – and, on the other side, an increasing inhibition or passive resistance in respect of the neutral stimuli, which ultimately issues in the establishment of a *negative* identification with them.

The positive identification with the conditioned stimulus, as we have said, is based on the assumption of the conditioned stimulus implying the unconditioned stimulus. Similarly, the *negative* identification with the "neutral" stimuli is based on a complementary assumption: *the negative assumption that these "neutral" stimuli do not imply the unconditioned stimulus.* This negative identification with stimuli still leaves the incipient form of identification more or less intact, for this latter is not based upon the assumption of a relation between sensory stimuli, but upon the assumption of the sensory stimulus itself. Because of this fact we call the incipient form "sensory identification," and the later form – based on the assumption of the relation of stimuli to the unconditioned stimulus – we call "abstract" or "emotional" identification. And "emotional identification" includes, as we have seen, "positive identification" and "negative identification."

Abstract or emotional identification is positive or negative according to whether it is based on a positive or negative assumption – i.e. according to whether the assumption on which it is founded affirms or denies a relation between stimuli. Since this type of assumption is, either way, concerned with the *relations* between sensory patterns or stimuli (patterns of patterns) we shall distinguish it from the mere assumption of sensory patterns in the same manner as we have distinguished between sensory stimuli (or sensory patterns) and abstract stimuli (or abstract patterns). Thus we have, also, sensory and abstract assumptions, of which the latter may be either positive or negative.

It will be noticed that our present conception of establishing a conditioned reflex is a considerable modification of the more usual one with which we started; it has become more akin to the conception of the process of discrimination which we briefly described on an earlier page. It may also be noticed that we have treated our subject only in relation to the conditioning of inborn reflexes which are concerned in the re-establishment of the absolute assumption and the emotion of pleasure. It will be clear upon consideration, however, that had we approached and pursued our subject in relation to the conditioning of those inborn reflexes which are concerned with the disestablishment of the absolute assumption and with the emotion of fear, we would have arrived at the present position though we traveled by a different route.

We can now envisage the environment of the individual as including a number of persons, animals, objects and ideas, with some of which he is positively identified – more or less strongly, as the case may be – and with others of which he is negatively identified – again, more or less strongly, as may be the particular case. These positive and negative identifications form a kind of series with two extremes which gradually merge towards the middle. In popular language, they form a sort of scale of likes and dislikes.

Emotional identification is, of course, familiar to psychoanalysis. But our conception of it differs somewhat from the psychoanalytic notion in being, as we believe, a more determinate conception, and in being considerably modified by our understanding of the process of assumption, from which identification is fundamentally derived.

Although psychoanalysis and all other branches and systems of psychology – in common with the rest of science and mental activities generally – are compelled continually to make assumptions and to base their whole superstructures upon an assumptive foundation, yet none of them make any provision at all for the actual part played in mental phenomena by the assumptive process. It is simply ignored. This is, perhaps, largely as it should be. For the study of the process of assumption and the recognition of its importance in mental life must necessarily remain the characteristic feature of a science of ideology and the intellect.

"Identification," says Freud, in his *Group Psychology and Analysis of the Ego*), "is known to psychoanalysis as the earliest expression of an emotional tie with another person. It plays a part in the early history of the Oedipus complex." And again: "... identification is the original form of emotional tie with an object... " He says, further: "We do not ourselves regard our analysis of identification as exhaustive... "

We may now broadly define emotional identification (positive and negative) as the feeling of dependence – for the re-establishment of the absolute assumption – upon some person, act, thing, idea or some collection, class, or group of these. In the case of negative identification the feeling of dependence will be negative. That is to say, the object of negative identification is rejected and repudiated – i.e. it is renounced; for it constitutes a limitation upon the re-establishment of the absolute assumption, and a limitation, moreover, which is recognised as such – though not recognised, as we shall soon see, as a *necessary* limitation. The object of negative identification, therefore, must be overcome, must be banished, must come to grief, be destroyed – or otherwise be removed as a limitation upon the assumption of self determinism. Equally, then, negative identification is a feeling of independence and it would seem better separately to define it so. But since there is a positive identification with the *removal* of the limitation – and this is precisely what constitutes a negative identification – then we can see that there is still involved a *dependence* upon the person (or other object of the identification) even though it means dependence upon his death, absence, degradation, defeat, or, according to the nature of the limitation, some other mode of its removal. From the foregoing it will be clear that, other things being equal, the more permanent the limitation, the stronger the negative identification (and emotional repudiation). It is clear, too, that positive and negative identification are not mutually exclusive, but rather, mutually interpenetrative and complementary.

The function of emotional identification can now easily be discerned: it is that of *"fixating"* modes of thinking and behaving. Instinctive or inborn reflex behaviour is fixed by an inherited and permanent nervous structure which will always work in more or less the same way in a given situation. Hence, for unconditioned reflex activity, emotions are superfluous and unnecessary. But for behaviour of the more intentional type, that type which depends upon the conditioned reflex and the plastic changeable activities of the cerebral cortex, emotional identification fulfills a useful – and indeed, completely necessary – function. *It serves to establish and fix the conditioned reflex.* Unless, on the part of Pavlov's dogs, there is a positive emotional identification with that stimulus which is the necessary condition for the presentation of the unconditioned stimulus, i.e. the giving of food – unless there is emotional identification with the assumption that a particular sensory pattern implies or signals food and the overcoming of the limiting internal stimulus of hunger – then, we suggest, no conditioned reflex can be established (or fixed) at all. This view of the basic function of emotion is further supported by the fact, mentioned above, that the animal which has had its cerebral hemispheres removed shows practically no sign of emotion.

Thus, like instinct and inborn reflex activity generally, the function and influence of emotional identification is of a conservative nature, making for the fixation of learnt behaviour and its underlying cognitive assumptions. Inspection of the human ideological field and a comparative study of ideologies serves but to confirm the conclusion that, in an ideology, the function of a system of emotional identifications is to fixate the main assumptive structure.

2.7 Development and Repression

W^E are now able to apply some of the results of the foregoing pages and describe in brief outline the main stages in the typical course of ideological development. In order to do this it will be convenient to choose the typical course of *ontogenetic* development, that is to say, the course of development pursued by the individual. There is every reason to believe, however, that – as in biological growth – the development of the individual broadly recapitulates, and sometimes extends, the series of evolutionary stages passed through by the group. This correlation of ontogeny and phylogeny in ideological development is forced upon us by a broad historical survey of the growth of religion, science, philosophy, politics etc., and the study of savage behaviour, on the one hand, and, on the other hand, by the study of the intellectual growth of the individual in modern society.

We shall distinguish two main and consecutive phases in the ideological development of a person: the first we shall call the *eido-static* phase, and the second we shall term the *eido-dynamic* phase. The earlier or eido-static phase begins approximately at birth and continues, through superstitious and primitive religious stages, well into the first stages of the scientific mode of thought. It embraces those modes of thought which are typical of mass social groups and therefore includes ideological levels which correspond successively with the typical ideological forms of political absolutism or fascism, conservatism and (towards the end of the phase) liberalism. The later or eido-dynamic phase proceeds from the first stages of scientific thinking and continues through more developed scientific stages. It includes modes of thought which are characteristic of intellectual social groups and contains, therefore, those ideological levels which successively correspond with typical ideological forms of socialism, communism and (towards the end of the phase) anarchism. Let us examine these two main phases of development more closely.

The eido-static phase begins, we have said, approximately at birth. It would be absurd, however, to suppose that the beginning of mental life corresponded with the comparatively sudden event of being born. During the period passed in sheltered seclusion of the womb, the nervous system of the individual is rapidly built up and differentiated; it is, moreover, active. Towards the latter end of the intra-uterine period certain sensory stimuli must penetrate the seclusion of the womb – both from the mother herself and from the more remote outside world – which are able to activate appropriate receptors and nerve paths in the nervous system of the unborn child. However, we must remember that in its womb-life the child has none of the urgent needs which it is to feel after birth, for all its bodily requirements are supplied by its mother. In the womb, therefore, there are no severe internal restraints or limitations (such as the stimulus of hunger) upon its inherited assumption of self-determinism. And, moreover, because of its sheltered position inside the mother's body, it is also protected from any severe limitations which would be otherwise imposed by intense external stimuli. Such vague sensory patterns as are actually received – e.g. rhythmic swaying from the mother's body –

movement, muffled sounds, maternal heartbeats, tactile sensations etc. – constitute no serious limitations upon the absolute assumption.

Nevertheless, we may suppose that *some* differentiation between stimuli, however little, actually occurs within the womb, especially towards the early stages of the unpleasant and painful birth-process. From the initial "tonic," or partial, inhibition of "neutral" stimuli, and the generalised sensory identification, develop the beginnings of emotional positive and negative identification. The more constant and familiar features of stimuli – e.g. rhythmic pattern – will get positively identified with the absolute assumption, and mild negative identification will therefore be developed towards the strange, occasional, more unfamiliar and disturbing intrusions into the monotonously rhythmic patterns. Thus it is suggested that the nascent stages of conditioning, assumption and identification begin *in utero*.

This primitive stage of intra-uterine bliss is recognised by psychoanalysis and is called the "feeling of unconditional omnipotence" by Ferenczi, who, I believe, was the first to draw attention to its importance. "In this state," he writes in his "Contributions to Psychoanalysis":

> the human being lives as a parasite of the mother's body. For the nascent being an 'outer world' exists only in a very restricted degree; all its needs for protection, warmth, and nourishment are assured by the mother. Indeed, it does not even have the trouble of taking the oxygen and nourishment that is brought to it, for it is seen to it that these materials, through suitable arrangements, arrive directly into its blood vessels. In comparison with this an intestinal worm, for example, has a good deal of work to perform, 'to change the outer world,' in order to maintain itself. All care for the foetus, however, is transferred to the mother. If, therefore, the human being possesses a mental life when in the womb, although only an unconscious one – and it would be foolish to believe that the mind begins to function only at the moment of birth – he must get from his existence the impression that he is in fact omnipotent. For what is omnipotence? The feeling that one has all one wants, and that one has nothing left to wish for. The foetus, however, could maintain this of itself, for it always has what is necessary for the satisfaction of its wants, and so has nothing to wish for, it is without wants.

With the onset of birth a radical change takes place. In the mental state of the child; for, in the process of being turned out of its shelter into a "hostile" world, its body is increasingly subjected to great physical constraint and painfully intense stimuli. There occurs an almost complete reversal of the state of affairs which previously existed *in utero*. The strange, new and intense stimuli now predominate over the monotonous and rhythmic patterns; and with the final emergence of the child, these latter are practically lost, they are no longer presented. A strong negative identification is rapidly developed toward these new and relatively intense stimuli, and soon after delivery the newborn babe exhibits this strong emotional rejection by violent uncoordinated motor reactions (struggling) and by crying. After experiencing further disagreeable sensations which continue to impose intense limitation upon the absolute assumption, the child is eventually pacified, as Ferenczi pointed out, by its being placed in a situation similar to the intra-uterine one. It is wrapped in soft, downy and warm coverings; it is placed where it is protected from intense optical, auditory and tactile stimuli; once again the muffled, monotonous and rhythmical patterns of stimuli are reproduced by gentle rocking movements and soft, low crooning sounds. These events induce the re-establishment of the absolute assumption: the limitation is overcome and the child passes into sleep, a condition which closely resembles the previous condition in the womb – to which latter state we give the name "self-identification" (i.e. the feeling of dependence upon the self).

Sooner or later the bodily needs of the infant make themselves felt. Once more intense somatic stimuli impose limitation upon (or "disestablish") the self -deterministic assumption. Again the child reacts by emotional rejection of the stimuli; once again it manifests motor reactions and cries. This situation eventually causes a teat to be placed in its mouth. When this is done the inborn sucking-reflex comes into operation, the infant imbibes, the limiting stimulus is gradually removed, and, with the re-establishment of the absolute assumption, sleep again intervenes. The series of events is continually repeated. So that before long, by the process of conditioning, the child comes to identify itself positively with certain sensory patterns which imply the unconditioned stimulus (teat in the mouth) and, through this, the re-establishment of the absolute assumption.

Thus, the infant comes eventually to "accept" the limitations imposed by certain comparatively intense stimuli which it previously would have rejected (e.g. those involved in its being handled or picked up for feeding, nursing, rocking etc.). However, it still emotionally rejects most other sensory patterns, particularly those of strong stimuli (such as loud noises and those involved when it is being changed, washed, bathed etc.) and continues to manifest its negative identification with these in the usual manner. (This is apart, of course, from those above – mentioned relatively soft and rhythmic patterns with which it is already strongly identified in the positive sense.)

As the child grows and its routine becomes more complex, chain conditioning proceeds apace. More and more limitations come to be accepted as, one after another, various sensory patterns and stimuli are assumed to imply the re-establishment of the absolute assumption. Similar conditioning also occurs, of course, with regard to the disestablishment of that assumption. Hence, after a period of time, the child has built up a structure of positive and negative assumptions to which it is more or less strongly attached by a corresponding system of positive and negative identifications of varying intensities. *But each new acceptance of a limitation can only be achieved in so far as the limitation is actually assimilated into or reconciled with the absolute assumption – i.e. in so far as it leads to the re-establishment of that assumption.* Each new acceptance of a limitation, therefore, involves the transformation of a negative assumption into a positive assumption and the transformation of a negative identification into a positive identification. Transformation also occurs in the other direction: that is to say, a limiting stimulus which has become "accepted" may cease to lead to re-establishment and, instead, lead to disestablishment. The positive assumption and identification are thus transformed into their negative counterparts. This takes place to some extent in the extinction or internal inhibition of a conditioned reflex.

Now, the process of transformation we have just described corresponds, not only to a form of inhibition, but also to the well-known process of repression originally discovered by Freud. That is to say, a negative identification is simply a "*repressed*" positive identification. And the strength of the negative identification is therefore proportional to the strength of the repression. Similarly, the positive identification (which, we have seen, results from the acceptance of a limitation and the inhibition of "passive resistance" – i.e. the inhibition of the inhibition of a stimulus) constitutes a form of "return of repressed material" – another familiar psycho-analytic concept. But "the return of repressed material," "the acceptance of a limitation," "the transformation of a negative into a positive identification" – which are all the same thing – necessarily involve the limitation, i.e. the repression, of the egoistic absolute assumption.

Thus we can now distinguish two kinds of repression: "internal" and "external." External repression is the repression of an external or objective limitation upon the egoistic assumption of self-determinism – in other words the repudiation or renunciation of the limit as a *necessary* and *positive* one. This is equivalent to the transformation of a positive into a negative identification (or assumption). "Internal repression," on the other hand, is the repression or limitation of the absolute assumption itself – i.e. it is the repression of an *unnecessary* and *negative* form of that assumption, a form which itself constitutes an internal or subjective limitation upon re-establishment. And this is equivalent to the transformation of a negative into a positive identification (or assumption). It can be seen from the foregoing that each kind of transformation or repression is but the inverse form of the other; and that each of the two types, in its occurrence, involves the simultaneous occurrence of its inverse type, but relative to opposite material or opposite kinds of limitation (i.e. either subjective or objective limitation). Moreover, it is the mutual interaction of internal and external repression – involved in the acceptance of objective and necessary limitations, and the rejection of subjective and unnecessary limitations – *which actually constitutes the intellectual and ideological development.*

Let us now return to the mental development of the child. The human infant remains helpless and dependent upon its parents or nurses for a relatively long period – a period which is unique among animals. We have seen that the child is nevertheless able to overcome limitations, and obtain its needs, by the simple method of displaying its emotional rejection of those limitations: that is, by motor reactions and crying. This mode of behaviour works tolerably well as a mode of resisting or overcoming limiting stimuli – especially in the earliest stages – so long as there are human beings to respond and minister to the infantile needs. The new-born infant soon comes to learn that these reactions are the necessary conditions for re-establishment, that they are the all-powerful password to success and satisfaction. The method soon becomes a kind of magic ritual; and here, indeed, We have the origin of magic, of magical ritual and passwords. And since religion and science have developed from magic, we have here, too, the very primeval roots and rudimentary beginnings of these.

But while this method of overcoming limitation works well in relation to the human part of the child's environment, it can have little success relative to the non-human organic or animal environment – and, of course, none at all in relation to the merely material and inorganic part of its environment. However, neither the child nor the primitive savage makes any such conscious distinctions. Whether the primitive mind accepts or rejects a limitation – whether it makes, in short, a positive or negative assumption – the reality or independence which it is forced to accord the limiting stimulus (human and non-human alike) is but the projection of its own nature, its own reality, its own assumption of independent, self-determined being. Nevertheless, a nascent distinction is at this stage beginning to appear in the primitive ideological structure. For though the projection of reality occurs for both types of assumption (and identification) – that is, positive and negative assumptions – the *kind* of reality which is projected in each case differs. And it differs according to whether the projection is that of the modified self which accepts certain limitations (the part of the self which is composed of the "returned material," the structure of assimilated positive assumptions and identifications – the de-repressed or conscious self) or whether the projection is that of the unmodified self which rejects limitations (the part of the self to which relates the "internally repressed" forms of the absolute assumption and the still "externally repressed" material: the negative assumptions and identifications – the unconscious or subconscious self).

Thus, because of this growing differentiation within the self (viz. the ideological structure) of a repressed part and a "returned" or "de-repressed" part, the reality which is accorded to stimuli relating to negative assumptions and identifications will differ from the reality which is given to stimuli pertaining to positive assumptions and identifications. The actual distinction which the child (or the savage) gradually comes to make between these stimuli, is the distinction between "good" and "bad" faithful projection of the child's own good and bad (or naughty) character. Inanimate objects which remain indifferent to the magic ritual of cries, whimpers, words, grimaces, gestures etc., or which frustrate the child's aims, are therefore wilfully "bad" and "naughty." On the other hand, those human beings who respond to the magical technique and minister to the child's aims, are "good" and well loved.

In actual practice, of course, the division is not so clean-cut. As the child is able to extend the magical technique to include the simple manipulation and control of certain objects – in short, as it is able to get about and do things for itself – the mental situation gets more complicated. For in learning to manipulate and control objects, the child is forced to accept more limitations which it previously rejected; de-repression or transformation from negative to positive assumption occurs. (De-repression or "return of repressed material" is, we have seen, equivalent to or concurrent with internal repression.) Objects are therefore good in so far as they respond to the extended magical technique of manipulation, and are bad and naughty in so far as they do not respond. Again, parents and nurses have by now begun to impose limitations upon the child's aims and behaviour in the form of certain prohibitions. In so far as these frustrations are resented, or not willingly accepted, then external repression occurs: i.e. the transformation of positive into negative assumptions and identifications. Those who impose the restrictions (parents, nurses, and later on, schoolmasters and others in authority) are therefore, in so far as the limitations are not accepted, "bad," "naughty," or evil. Nevertheless, despite this growing ambivalence towards humans and non-human objects, the ideological structure of the child (and of the savage, too) is such that, on the whole, the positive assumptions and identifications are generally orientated towards persons and people, whereas the negative assumptions and identifications are orientated towards non-human and inanimate objects. The primitive mind, therefore, owing to its inability to understand and control material objects – or, what is the same thing, because of the material object's frustration of its aims is repressed with respect to the inanimate world in general. This external repression (which is, as we have seen, the emotional rejection of an objective limit) manifests itself as a tendency towards a general repudiation of matter and a predisposition or predilection for refusing to recognise its determining influence. The attitude is well known to exist among primitive and savage peoples and, in its more developed forms, characterises the outlook of the majority of people in modern civilised communities. Inanimate matter is regarded as of evil significance. In the case of the child and the savage, however, the "evil" (or frustrating) nature of the inanimate object is attributed to a wilfull, intractable spirit: a projection of their own internally repressed and "evil" ("bad" or "naughty") nature.

The recognition of this external repression in relation to the inorganic material world, *as a characteristic feature of the primitive intellect*, is vital for the understanding of ideological development. For, as mentioned above, ideological growth largely depends upon the interaction of internal and external repression. And in these early stages of development the ideological structure shows quite clearly the broad division of its assumptions and identifications into two main groups: one of which (the externally repressed, sub-conscious or negative group) is orientated towards the inanimate world of matter, and the other of which (the de-repressed, conscious, or positive group) is orientated towards human society. Although it undergoes considerable modification in further stages of development, this basic orientation of the ideological structure remains fundamentally the same throughout most of the eido-static phase. Moreover, it provides us with the key to the understanding of the so called herd instinct and the formation of social groups; for we now see that there is a two-fold compulsion on the primitive individual: one, positive, and drawing him into association with humans, and the other, negative, driving him away from isolation or association with inanimate nature. Hence, most humans, especially children and primitive people, have a great dislike, or even fear, of being alone, of being isolated from the social group with only inanimate non-human being for company. Such is the individual's attachment to the human group that he will accept the severest limitations and prohibitions imposed by group – life rather than quit his fellows for a life of solitary independence. Each individual seeks independence only within the confines of the social group. *We can now quite easily discern the origin of the universal fear or dread of offending the group, of the fear of public opinion, and of the urge of of the mass towards conformity.*

In the case of the small child, the social group, of course, begins with the mother and then extends to the father and to the rest of the family. In the same way as we have seen the projection in negative assumption to be the projection of the child's "bad" self, so we find that the projection in positive assumption is the projection of the child's "good" self – i.e. the conscious de-repressed and modified self. This is the self – or that part of the ideological structure – which accepts limitations; it is therefore not only the self in which resides all the virtues but also the self which is the more successful in overcoming limitations and the more capable of exercising control. Hence, when the child positively identifies itself with its parents (or with later authorities, with heroes and leaders of the social group) it is not only projecting its own more virtuous nature, but also its more successful, capable, and powerful nature as well. Within the family circle, therefore, the child will most strongly identify itself with the most powerful and capable member: usually, of course, the father. The strength of other positive identifications made with the rest of the family will also largely depend upon the rank and power of each particular member. It can easily be seen that this hierarchy of identifications sets the pattern for a great deal of behaviour later on in larger social groups: in school, in the army, in business, in political life etc. It is this strong positive identification with the group and with rank, power, leadership, heroes and authority, on the one hand, and the strong negative identification with material nature on the other which predispose youthful, ignorant and primitive minds to identify themselves with the mass ideology of fascism.

As the child grows and the ideological development proceeds - greatly assisted by the processes of more or less organised education – the animistic stage in mental growth (in which inanimate objects are invested with the infant's projection of self-determinism) is rapidly and considerably modified. We have seen that in the primitive animistic ideological structure there appeared an incipient dualism. Originally, all objects, human and non-human alike, were emotionally rejected. Then, when the somatic needs of the newborn infant imposed greater limitations upon its self-deterministic assumption than those imposed by external stimuli, the child was forced to accept those limitations which led to re-establishment. It continued, however, to reject those external stimuli which led to disestablishment and frustration. The child thus built up a primitive structure of positive and negative assumptions and identifications which became broadly divided, so that the positive structure directly related to human beings and the negative structure related to inanimate nature. The nascent dualism to which we wish to draw attention concerns the projection of selfdeterminism into the inanimate object.

At first no very clear distinction is made between the object itself and the self-deterministic spirit which pervades it. Later, however, after much investigation of the object (largely brought about by the obsessive interest and intense pre-occupation with material objects caused by the external repression) the child comes to make the distinction – based on analogy with itself – between the obvious and determined exterior of objects, and their mysterious and self-determining interior; between the sensory patterns of matter and the inherent force which resists and frustrates the child. It wishes to see "inside" the object. It wants to pull things to pieces. After much further experience in the manipulation of objects, and not finding "inside" them what it is unconsciously seeking, it comes, in the process, to accept further limitations imposed by the nature of matter, and thus is able to master the object and satisfy its intense curiosity. The object no longer frustrates it as before. Re-establishment occurs; and so, therefore, does transformation of negative to positive assumptions. The de-repressed or returned material, with its corresponding internal repression, along with the newly introjected limitation – the abstract stimuli – *constitutes the individual's increased understanding.* The de-repression (and concurrent internal repression) constitutes, in other words, the assimilation into the ideological structure of the newly assumed mutual relations between sensory stimuli.

This increased understanding and control of the material object purges it of its inner, mysterious, intractable and indeterministic spirit. The purging process, however, is limited and not complete, for the very simple reason that the individual's understanding and control of the object remains limited and incomplete. The inherent self-determinism or indeterministic nature of inanimate objects remains in the form of mysterious, intractable forces which, in so far as they are not understood and controlled, are regarded as responsible for chance, accident, luck or ill-luck. Success or failure in any aim or enterprise thus comes to depend upon whether these mysterious inherent forces are favouribly or unfavouribly disposed towards the individual. (This attitude is essentially that which is typical of the many millions in modern society who "believe in luck" or who are obsessively preoccupied with betting, gambling and other forms of speculation upon chance.)

Again, the purging process begins with the depersonification of self-determinism only in the most familiar, investigated and immediate of inanimate object. The more remote and inaccessible objects, associated with large-scale and more mysterious phenomena, retain their spiritual or personified counterparts for much longer. Moreover, as the understanding and depersonification of the individual's immediate material surroundings proceed, and the fundamental distinction or dualism between mind and matter becomes more and more manifest, these remoter spirits become progressively more detached and distinguished from their material abodes. They thus become capable of leaving their dwelling-places in trees, rivers, mountains etc. and of acting and exerting their mysterious powers elsewhere. Unencumbered by the shackles of gross materiality, these disembodied spirits – beneficent or malevolent according to whether they aid or frustrate the individual – exercise their capricious, whimsical, fancy-free, indeterministic (i.e. magical) control over mere material things by spoken commands and incantations, by ritualistic behaviour and gestures. They disappear, they assume many and various forms, they span great distances in an instant; and mundane material objects, like craven slaves, obey their least commands in a flash. It is all so patent that these miraculous and omnipotent powers over matter are nothing but projections of internally repressed forms of the self deterministic or absolute assumption.

This conception of the more remote and ultimate nature of the material world or universe (any individual's conception of which we call his "*cosmic situation*") results, as we have said, from the externally repressed limitations of matter upon the absolute assumption, on the one hand, and the internally repressed forms of that assumption, on the other. Internal repression, we saw, originally referred to the individual's relation to the social group and its members (his conception of which we call the "*group situation*"). It will be obvious that projection in the "cosmic situation" provides a kind of compensation for the limitations upon and frustrations of the absolute assumption actually suffered in the group and in contact with matter. Again, it will be evident that the cosmic situation is largely influenced by the individual's organisation of the group situation. These two trends become plainer as the individual progresses further from the animistic stage into dualistic idealism.

With the fuller appearance of this latter stage of the cosmic situation, the depersonification of the material world is almost complete. The indeterministic spiritual realm is divested of much of its former parochial character and largely divorced from the material universe. It is an abode for the departed of everlasting bliss if they were "good" and accepted the limitations imposed by the group, and of everlasting punishment if they were "wicked" and rejected the group restrictions. The organisation of the spirits is upon a large-scale family basis, with an omnipotent Spirit at the head of the family hierarchy who is regarded as the Father and Creator of all things and especially of all men, who are His children. The other side of this dualistic cosmic situation shows that, with the more or less complete separation of the spiritual or self-deterministic realm from the material universe, the way is left open for the development of those early modes of scientific thinking which concern the mechanistic behaviour of matter.

The group situation corresponding to this dualistic stage is typified in the conservative mode of thought. Here again, the social life of the nation and of the group of nations is interpreted largely in terms of the assumptions and identifications of typical family life. The adored monarch, president, or other head of the state, is regarded as the virtuous and powerful head of the national family or empire (family of nations). The king is the father of his people; he is the symbol of the national group, the members of which are related by blood-ties, and a symbol, also, of the whole body of group restrictions – i.e. the constitution or *status quo*. The hierarchy of identifications characteristic of the earlier group situation of family life, and later of larger groups, is finally transferred to the whole national group itself. The national heroes, past and present, are thus modifications and adaptations of the earlier matter – and later father-identification "Motherland," "fatherland," "mother-country," mother-tongue," "John Bull," "Britannia" etc. are words and symbols of a type especially recurrent in conservative thought. "What was good enough for my father is good enough for me" is the traditional conservative sentiment. Other nations, especially those with origins and histories more in common with one's own, are "our cousins," "our brothers" or "sister-nations." Political merit for the conservative consists in the preservation of the "good," i.e. those hierarchic institutions which express his cosmic and group situations. "God, King and Country (or Empire)" is thus the watch ward and quintessence of the conservative attitude. Those who are politically "good" and" right" are those who accept and preserve the continuity of the group limitations; those who are "bad" or "wrong" are those who reject the group restrictions and traditions and who rebel against the group. (Here, of course, the Oedipus complex, discovered and described by Freud, plays its part.) The conservative outlook or group situation is thus to be interpreted in terms of the earlier group situation into which the individual was largely driven by his external repression of the objective limitations imposed by inanimate matter.

Further progress in the ideological development leads from the cosmic situation of "dualistic idealism" to that of "mechanistic materialism." We saw that the progressive separation of the indeterministic spiritual realm from the material world followed upon an increasing understanding of the way matter works – in other words, upon depression of the externally repressed objective limitations imposed by matter. As the individual's knowledge grows concerning, on the one hand, the physical nature of the mare remote universe and, on the other, concerning the mechanical, physical and chemical nature of organic matter, the process of depersonificatian of the universe proceeds through its last stages towards its limit. At that limit the dualism of spirit and matter (of self-determinism and determinism) becomes absolute: that is to say, side by side with the growing understanding *that the material world is not composed of fundamentally different types of being but is composed of one fundamental type*, there: occurs a similar breaking-up of the different beings of the indeterministic spiritual world into one basic type – a type of being which can have no material characteristics whatever and which has no existence inside space and time. Thus, self-determinism in the farm of spirit or mind is isolated or eliminated from the material universe. It requires but one more step really to complete the process and make the separation of spirit and matter absolute; *and that is to regard indeterministic spirit or mind as entirely non-existent.* For in possessing existence spirit has something in common with matter, and depersonification therefore remains incomplete. The final step annihilates the conscious dualism and leads directly to mechanistic materialism.

The gradual approach and development of this cosmic situation of the individual reacts on his group situation. His increasing understanding of the mechanistic nature of the universe necessarily involves depression – i.e. the acceptance of progressively more limitations upon the absolute assumption; it involves, in short, further internal repression. He is becoming less and less externally repressed with respect to the nature of inanimate matter; he no longer believes in spirits or other apparitions; he no longer fears being alone with inanimate matter and his own thoughts. He is thus no longer impelled by a strong negative identification with matter into the refuge of strong positive identification with the primitive group. On the contrary, the family group, with its permanent hierarchic structure, its traditional taboos, sentiments, etc., becomes a fetter upon the individual's new-won freedom and independence in the cosmic situation. The conservative group situation – which, with its hierarchy of identifications with power and success, assumes the fundamental inborn inequality of men and their innate division into permanent and qualitatively distinct levels of classes – becomes incompatible with the new assumptions, derived from the individual's cosmic situation, of the fundamental qualitative sameness and equality of all being.

Alongside, therefore, with the development of the new cosmic situation, there develops a growing rejection of those assumptions and identifications which are essentially characteristic of the conservative outlook and way of life. A new ideological level is emerging that begins to express itself in terms which challenge the former assumptions of pre-ordained, innate and permanent hierarchy of all human and material nature. Transferring from the cosmic to the group situation the general ideas of universal change and natural development, the individual now begins to call for "Progress," "Reform" and "Social Change." The conservation of a more or less rigid unchangeable hierarchic social structure becomes a shackle upon the progress and development of the members of society, particularly those of the "lower orders." "Freedom of the Individual," "Tolerance," "Liberty of the People," thus become additional watch-words with the emergence of this newer stage in ideological development: a stage which is everywhere typified in the liberal mode of thought.

With the further growth of the deterministic and scientific view of the material universe, and the approach of the individual's cosmic situation towards the philosophy of mechanistic materialism, the liberal group situation ripens into maturity. And with the full onset of these latter stages of growth the eido-static phase draws to its close. Simultaneously with this recession there occurs an ever-increasing positive identification of the individual with the principles (or assumptions) of universal change and determinism. In the cosmic and group situations of the eido-static phase all objects and entities of the external world – human and non-human alike – are given the status of independent, self-determined things in themselves, undergoing only such changes as do not alter their different qualitative natures, which latter remain, therefore, fixed, static and absolute. With the approach and advent of the eido-dynamic phase, however, the absolute status of each separate entity disappears. As the deterministic principle becomes more and more enthroned in the cosmic situation the assumption of, the independent and self-deterministic nature of entities gives way to the assumption of their complete dependence and relativity.

The final ascendancy and supremacy of the assumption of determinism coincides, as we have seen, with the complete elimination of self-determinism from the material universe – i.e. with the final internal repression of the assumption of self-determinism. Subjective mind ceases to exist; objective matter alone is real. For the mechanistic materialist, therefore, the principle of universal change or development can strictly apply only to the qualitative changes in the forms of objective material entities and beings. Hence, in the later stages of the liberal group situation, which typically come under the sway of the deterministic principle and mechanistic materialism, the liberal intellectual can still have no conception of a real, independent social evolution – i.e. an evolution involving not only qualitative changes of the material entities within the social organism, but involving also a series of fundamental qualitative changes of the whole social organism itself. Such social changes and reforms of the social structure which the liberal advocates, and with which he is emotionally identified, still leave the fundamental quality of the social and economic system – its hierarchic or class structure – as it was. The liberal does not advocate the abolition of capitalism with its inevitable hierarchy of economic categories, but rather the abolition of the conservative rigidity of that structure. All men must have an equal opportunity to raise themselves in the social structure; the common or poor man must have an equal opportunity to better himself; the hierarchic structure must become more fluid.

The foregoing is approximately the position at the outset of the eido-dynamic phase of development. The fuller and more definite growth of this phase involves the transition from the liberal to the socialist group situation, during which it becomes increasingly evident that the whole ideological structure is undergoing a major and fundamental re-orientation. We saw how, in the early part of the eido-static phase, the ideological structure was broadly divided so that its negative assumptions and identifications related to the non-human material world (the cosmic situation) and its positive assumptions and identifications related to human beings (the group situation). In other words, the primitive mind is externally repressed with respect to its cosmic situation and internally repressed with respect to its group situation. The negative identification with inanimate nature results from frustration, or "disestablishment," in dealing with matter, and produces (a) the cosmic projection of forms of self-determinism which are internally repressed and (b) an obsessive interest in matter and in overcoming its limiting influence.

This state of affairs, we saw, became altered as understanding grew of the material world. As more and more of the limitations imposed by matter came to be accepted, transformation from negative to positive assumptions and identifications occurred. The growing mind became progressively less externally repressed with respect to the material world, and progressively more internally repressed with respect to it. The new growth led to the gradual isolation of the projected self determinism from the material world until, when the process of depersonification became complete, the absolute or self-deterministic assumption was completely repressed and expunged from the universe and from the mind. The deterministic assumption, derived from increasingly successful experience with matter, finally became enthroned in consciousness. The development of the cosmic situation, however, reacted upon the group situation. The rigid hierarchic structure of the group, together with the ideology which maintains and perpetuates it, becomes a fetter upon the individual's development and begins to frustrate him. Transformation from positive to negative assumptions occurs, therefore, in respect of the existing group structure and the group modes of thought which support it. These latter become, in a word, intellectually and emotionally rejected. The individual (now separated from the mass group as an independent intellectual) *has now become internally repressed with respect to the cosmic situation and has become externally repressed with respect to the group situation.*

This eido-dynamic re-orientation of the ideological structure is a complete reversal of the orientation in the early part of the eido-static phase. The earlier eido-static orientation resulted in the projection of subjective self-determinism into the material world. When, later, self-determinism was separated from each and every object, finally repressed and expunged from the universe in favour of the deterministic principle, every object and entity became completely determined and relative. But this, of course, is only another way of regarding the material world as an entirely objective whole, independent, self-contained, self-determined, absolute and complete in itself. Thus the whole universe of relative, changing, determined and objective beings becomes itself a form of self-determinism – an absolute, constant and real objectivity, a reality completely independent of mind.

Now, we have learnt that, in the eido-dynamic re-orientation of the ideological structure, the individual becomes externally repressed in relation to the group. The earlier eido-static projection of subjective forms of self-determinism no longer occurs. But the mere exchange of the group situation for the cosmic situation as the sphere in which external repression operates, does not, of course, end the necessity of projection. In the same way that negative identification with matter resulted in the projection of self-determinism in its subjective form, so now, in the new phase – with its transposition of the cosmic and group situations – the negative identification with the group structure results in the projection of self-determinism, *but in its objective form of complete and absolute determinism.*

With this projection the individual now comes to regard the group structure as determined, not by the subjective and illusory ideas of the group members, but by quite independent objective laws and processes – particularly and ultimately economic laws and processes. By the operation of these same basic laws the group structure is changing and developing. For, as the minds of people are all *equally* and *wholly* determined by material conditions and do not determine themselves, as ideas and ideologies are but reflections of the objective world, then *the large-scale and fundamental changes in the material economic conditions must necessarily produce fundamental ideological changes on a mass scale.* Since these fundamental ideological changes must inevitably bring about an increasing understanding and rejection of the existing social structure on the part of the huge majority which occupies the inferior position in that structure, then the class or hierarchic nature of society is finally doomed to extinction by the concerted action of the masses. Human society is, therefore, developing towards a classless social order, in which all individuals shall be free and equal, in which wealth is produced for the use of all and not for the enrichment and power of the few, and in which the whole of the people shall own and control society for the benefit of all. The ideologies which support the class nature of society will fade away and become as extinct as the dodo. The classless society is therefore objectively self-determined and ideologically homogeneous.

Thus does our individual arrive, in his ideological development, at the socialist group situation. In the eido-static phase the subjective form of self-determinism was projected as a separate spiritual realm in which deterministic matter no longer frustrated the individual. It was a kind of compensation for the limitations and frustrations actually suffered. So, too, we see, in the eido-dynamic phase, there occurs a projection into the future, of the objective form of self-determinism – i.e. the objectively self-determined and rational social order. This, too, is a form of compensation for the actual limitations and frustrations suffered by the socialist intellectual in his relations with the group and its obstinate and persistent identifications with personal power, wealth, success, hierarchy, authority, leadership, "bosses" etc. *In essence this projection is his own objective and deterministic attitude projected into the group.*

Further development in the eido-dynamic phase leads more and more to the frustration of the intellectual in respect of the actual group and its dominant ideologies. The new growth leads, by successive stages similar to those we have already described, first to the communist group situation and then to that of the anarchist. As this occurs the intellectual develops stronger and stronger negative identification with the existing group structure; he becomes more obsessively interested in it and studies its origin and growth with increasing assiduity. The study of the group reacts upon his cosmic situation and this develops, from mechanistic and evolutionary materialism, to "dialectical materialism" – in which latter the repressed self-deterministic assumption partially returns to consciousness in the form of the dialectic principle, as the universal principle of all forms of change and motion.

However scientific he may be with regard to the study of material conditions and development, the intellectual's strong and increasing emotional repudiation of existing class society, and his equally strong and increasing emotional sympathy for the projected classless society, prevent him from gaining a proper and adequate understanding of the masses and of the real nature of their characteristic ideology. For the violent emotional repudiation of the class or hierarchic structure extends to the "upper" or "capitalist" class, with whom that structure is associated. Similarly, the strong emotional sympathy or positive identification with the projected classless society extends to the "lower," or "working," class, who are associated with that society. The mass ideologies which perpetuate and support class society thus become identified with the capitalist class, who tend to become the repository of all that is vicious, machiavellian and irrational. The intellectual ideologies, on the other hand, become identified with the working class, with the masses themselves, who become thereby the repository for all that is socially healthy, virtuous, intelligent and rational.

This growing and "irreconcilable" dualism (between the existing society and the projected society) within the group situation of the eido-dynamic phase is a similar and complementary growth to the earlier dualism (between the existing world and the projected world) which developed in the cosmic situation of the eido-static phase – i.e. in dualistic idealism. In the eido-static phase the dualism was finally overcome by the increasing study and understanding of the material world. So, too, with the dualism within the group situations of the eido-dynamic

phase: it can only be finally overcome by the further scientific study of the group –
i.e. its *ideological* nature.

2.8 Conclusion

THE point has now been reached from which this book really sets out. That is to say, we have now reached, in our account, that stage in the intellectual development of the individual where his further progress depends on his recognition of an independent, self-determined ideological domain – i.e. as a domain, realm or class of phenomena which, because it exhibits, its own characteristic laws, processes, mechanisms, interrelations and interactions peculiar to itself, has therefore a large measure of independence (or, what is the same, *internal* dependence, or self-determinism); and which, because of its interaction with other classes of phenomena, partly determines and, at the same time, is partly determined by, these latter.

It entails his recognition of *ideological form* (as distinct from mere recognition of ideological content or subject-matter) and, also, an understanding of the various ideological forms as *systematically and fundamentally* related – as comprising, in fact: (a) a chronological succession of typical stages in the evolution of intellect and (b) a permanent hierarchic structure of coexistent, interacting and mutually-dependent levels of intellectual development.

Owing to the increasing frustration of his social or group aims (by the obstinate but inevitable persistence of the mass modes of thought, i.e. political collectivism) – owing, in other words, to the signal lack of success attending his efforts to universalise his own ideological form (that of political individualism) the intellectual is driven into ascribing an ever-increasing duration to the period between present society and the coming of the projected classless society. The self-determined, classless society, in short, recedes more and more into the remote and indefinite future – just as, in the earlier eido-static phase, the self-deterministic spirit world receded further into space, away from immediate reality, and became progressively more indefinite and indeterminate. Again, as was also the case with the earlier recession, the process eventually approaches a point beyond which the projection becomes so removed from immediate reality that it ceases to have any real value or practical significance. Accordingly, the intellectual's strong emotional identification with the classless society and its underlying mass-rationality assumption becomes gradually weakened. His own emotional and irrational "faith" in the masses (i.e., in their development *en masse* towards political individualism) eventually becomes shaken and undermined. The intellectual is thus, by his growing scepticism, increasingly brought to the position of having to turn his attention to the ideological limitations of the mass group – to interest himself in ideological forms and the process of ideological development itself.

In so doing he comes to understand the ideological domain as no mere impotent by-product of the economic process and of other material processes, but as including these processes in qualitatively new interconnections, sequences and interactions – constituting a relatively new class of phenomena, a higher and more complex level of activities: exhibiting laws, processes etc. of its own and therefore possessing a great measure of *real* internal dependence and self-determinism.

Once this further development of his scientific attitude has really begun, the individual rapidly proceeds to rid himself, one after another, of many other unwarrantable prejudices and assumptions. For ideological science must be, above all, the rational, objective study of these prejudices and assumptions – its most distinctive feature being the recognition of the assumptive and identification processed as fundamental for comprehending the nature and growth of intellect. In proportion as his understanding of ideological phenomena develops, the intellectual no longer has the same need of illusory ideological projections of self-determinism *beyond* the world of reality, for he has at last found and recognised the self-deterministic principle operating in the immediately-present world within and around him.

No longer is his position that everything is merely, purely or *absolutely* determined – that is, determined *exclusively* and *solely* from without, by something *else*; his understanding, now, is that, besides being determined from without, all things – in so far as they possess structure, in so far as they are composed of interacting, mutually-dependent parts and process-levels – are also, to *some* extent, *self*-regulating, independent and self-determined; and that, the more the material parts and functions of structures – by virtue of their mutual determination and interdependence – are integrated into further groups of interacting parts and functions belonging to higher and more complex process-levels, the more are these structures actually, and in fact, self-determined.

Such, broadly speaking, are the main changes in the individual's outlook (or, rather, in his cosmic situation) which arise from the study and understanding of the ideological domain.

Only when this study and understanding of the ideological nature of groups is accomplished by a sufficient number of the more scientifically-minded members of the community, will the scientific *and – at the same time – democratic* control of the group become possible as a really practicable proposition.

With the development of scientific knowledge of the various ideologies or ideological levels, and of the different orientations of their underlying structures of positive-negative assumptions and identifications, it becomes possible to apply this knowledge in the sphere of education, publicity, propaganda, and in social and political relations generally. Progressive and socially-useful policies, aims, ideas etc., of the broader, more inclusive kind, can henceforth be presented to an ideological group in terms of their particular structure of assumptions and identifications, with the practical certainty of acceptance and agreement by the majority within that group.

Human society, with the aid of science and the deterministic principle, has largely conquered the limitations and problems imposed upon it by material nature. But the large-scale application of science in industrial and economic life has served merely to bring to the fore-front the increasing ideological problems imposed by human nature. With the aid of science and the self-deterministic principle, these problems, too, may eventually be conquered. Human society would then be master, not only of inanimate nature, but of itself.

Part III

New Material

Bibliography

The most likely sources for quotations found in Walsby's book.

Bacon, Francis: *Instauratio Magna* (1620) .

Baldwin, Earl: *On England* (London: Philip Allan, 1926).

Banks, Sir R. M.: *Conservative Outlook, The* (London: Chapman and Hall, 1929).

Brady, Robert A.: *Spirit and Structure of German Fascism, The* (London: V. Gollancz, 1937).

Brogan, Colm: *Who are 'the People'?* (London: Hollis and Carter, 1944).

Brumwell, J. R. M.: *This Changing World* (London: G. Routledge, 1944).

Bruck, Arthur Moeller van den: *Germany's Third Empire* (London: George Allen & Unwin, 1934).

Burnham, James: *Managerial Revolution, The* (Harmondsworth: Penguin, 1941).

Chakotin, Serge: *Rape of the Masses, The* (New York: Fortean, 1940).

Chamberlain, William Henry: *Collectivism* (New York: The Macmillan Company, 1937).

Cecil, Lord Hugh: *Conservatism.*

Concise Oxford Dictionary, The (Oxford: Oxford University, 1944).

Daily Telegraph, The, 14 June 1945.

Drennan, James: *B.U.F.: Oswald Mosley and British Fascism* ([London]: Murray, 1934).

Eddington, Sir Arthur: *New Pathways in Science* (Cambridge: University Press, 1935).

Eddington, Sir Arthur: *Philosophy of Science, The* (Cambridge: Cambridge University Press, 1939).

Enciclopedia Italiana 14th Edition (London: Hogarth Press, 1932).

Engles: *Ludwig Feuerbach* (1886).

Ferenczi, Sandor: *Further Contributions to the Theory and Technique of Psycho-analysis* (London: Hogarth, 1926).

Freud, Sigmund: *Group Psychology and the Analysis of the Ego* (New York: Boni and Liveright, 1921).

Freud, Sigmund: *New Introductory Lectures on Psycho-analysis* (London: Hogarth Press, 1933).

Gangulee, Nagendranath.: *Mind and Face of Nazi Germany, The* (London: John Murray, 1942).

Haldane, John Burdon Sanderson: *Marxist Philosophy and the Sciences, The* (New York: Random House, 1939).

Hegel, Georg *Phenomenology of Mind, The* (1807).

Hegel, Georg: *Science of Logic, The* (1830).

Heiden, Konrad: *Hitler* (1936).

Heiden, Konrad: *One Man Against Europe* (Harmondsworth: Penguin Books, 1939). '

Holland, Thomas (ed): *Science in the Changing World* (George Allen And Unwin Limited 1933).

International Journal of Ethics, Vol. 23, No. 4 (July 1913).

Jung, Carl: *Integration of the Personality* (New York: Farrar & Rinehart, 1939).

Knickerbocker, H. R.: *Is Tomorrow Hitler's?* (New York: Reynal and Hitchcock, 1941).

Koestler, Arthur: "Yogi and the Commissar, The" in *Russian Review*, Vol. 5, No. 1 Autumn, 1945.

Le Bon, Gustave: *Crowd, The* (1895).

McDougall, William: *Frontiers of Psychology* (Cambridge: Cambridge University Press, 1934).

McDougall, William: *Group Mind, The* (New York: Putman, 1920).

McDougall, William: *World Chaos* (London: Kegan Paul, Trench, Trubner & Co., 1932).

Mannheim, Karl: *Ideology and Utopia* (London: Kegan Paul, Trench, Trubner & Co., 1936).

Marx, Karl: *German Ideology, The* (1932).

Marx, Karl and Friedrich Engles: *B. Selected Correspondence 1846-1895 with Commentary and Notes* (Lawrence & Wishart, London 1934).

Mussolini, Benito : *My Autobiography* (New York: Charles Scribner's Sons 1928).

Mussolini, Benito : *Political and Social Doctrine of Fascism, The* (London: Hogarth Press, 1933).

Nature (18 January 1936).

Popolo d'Italia (22 November 1921).

Prezzolini, Giuseppe: *Fascism* (New York: E. P. Dutton, 1926).

Rader, Melvin: "No Compromise" in *Review of Politics, The*, Vol. 1, No. 4 (October 1939).

Read, Herbert: *Philosophy of Anarchism, The* (London: Freedom Press 1940).

Rocker, Rudolf: *Anarcho-Syndicalism* (London: Martin Secker and Warburg Ltd., 1938).

Russell, Bertrand: *Let the People Think* (London: London, Rationalist Press Association, 1941).

Spencer, Herbert: *First Principles* (New York: D. Appleton and Company, 1897).

Waddington, C. H.: "Scientific Attitude, The" in *Philosophy of Science*, Vol. 16, No. 3 (July, 1949).

Whitaker's Almanack (London: J. Whitaker's and Sons, 1945).

War Commentary, (19 [Month?] 1945).

Selected Citations

Published works that cite *The Domain of Ideologies*.

Social Science Bulletin Special Issue 1 January 1948 ("We have just received [...] a small delivery of Walsby's *Domain of Ideologies*...").

Tribune, 30 January 1948 ("Special Review of Walsby's *Domain of Ideologies*").

Tribune, 6 February 1948 ("Harold Walsby's *Domain of Ideologies*").

"A Domain Still Unexplained" by George Woodcock from *Freedom*, 21 February 1948.

"Review" by Richard Tatham from *Science & Ideology* 1, March 1948.

"Science and Anarchism" by Richard Tatham from *Science & Ideology* 2, April 1948.

"A Sociologist at Large" by Lan Freed from *Rationalist Press Association Literary Guide*, May 1948.

"The Importance of Evidence" by Richard Tatham from *Science & Ideology* 4, June 1948.

The American Political Science Review, Vol. 42, No. 3, June 1948, page 631 ("Recent publications of political interest).

"Review" by H. H. Preece from *The Free Thinker*, 15 August 1948.

"The Basis for Action" from *Science & Ideology* 7, September 1948.

New Statesman, Volume 8, Issue 355, 1948.

British Book Bews by the British Council, 1948.

The Sociological Review, Volume 40, 1948.

The Left Forum, 1948.

The Dublin Magazine, Volumes 23-24 by Seumas O'Sullivan, 1948.

The Oxford Magazine Volume 67, 1948.

Wales Volume 8 Issues 29-30 by Druid Press, 1948.

Foreign Affairs, Volume 27 by the Council on Foreign Relations, 1949.

"Review" from *Universum* 3, 20 March 1949.

Infantry Journal, Volumes 64-65, 1949.

"The Domain of Sterilities" by Gilmac from *The Socialist Standard*, April 1949.

"Mugwump and Moonshine" by Harold Walsby, circa 1949.

Report of the 20th Meeting of the 46th Editorial Committee. 17 May 1949. ("Editorial Committee asked the EC to endorse their action in not publishing a 4,000 word reply received from the SSA of the criticism published in the [*Socialist Standard*] of the book *Domain of Ideologies* and to publish a short statement in the [*Socialist Standard*] dealing with this matter. Resolution: Cash and Waters 'That the recommendation of the Editorial Committee be accepted.' Agd.).

Heaven and Communism by P. J. Rollings from *The Socialist Leader*, 25 March 1950.

Fundamentals of World Organization by Werner Levi, 1950.

Public Opinion Quarterly, Vol. 19, No. 1, Spring 1955.

The Reading Standard, May 4 1956.

Social Control by Joseph Slabey Rouček, 1956.

Democracy, Ideology, and Objectivity by Arne Næss, 1956.

152

On Not Being Able to Paint by Marion Blackett Milner, 1958.
Midwest Journal of Political Science, Volumes 4-5, 1960.
Midwest Journal of Political Science, Vol. 5, No. 4, Novenber 1961.
Ideologie by Jürgen Frese, 1965.
Individualism and Nationalism in American Ideology by Yehoshua Arieli, 1966.
Guide to Reference Materials in Political Science Volume 1 by Lubomyr Roman Wynar, 1968.
Idee und Ideologie by Erwin Hölzle, 1969.
The Failure of Elites by Frank Bonilla, 1970.
Ideological Tendencies Within Chilean Christian Democracy by Michael Fleet, 1972.
Marxism, Communism, and Western Society edited by Claus Dieter Kernig, 1973.
The Science of You by John Rowan, 1973.
The Social Individual by John Rowan, 1973.
Psychological Aspects of Society by John Rowan, 1973.
Systematics Volume 11 by Coombe Spring Press, 1973.
Mr. Jinnah as a Political Thinker by Shafique Ali Khan, 1974.
The Sociology of Karl Mannheim by Gunter W. Remmling, 1975.
The Monument by Robert Barltrop, 1975.
"Draft Introduction for an intended second edition" by Peter Shepherd circa 1976.
Myth, Symbolic Modes and Ideology by Albert B. Friedman, 1976.
Ideologie & Wissenschaft - Gesellschaft by Hans-Joachim Lieber, 1976.
Critique épistémologique de l'analyse systémique de David Easton by Denis Monière,1976.
An Outline Sketch of Systematic Ideology by George Walford, 1977.
Peter Hunot: Ideology Before Walsby, Some Notes on Karl Mannheim's Work on Ideology by Peter Shepherd, March 1979.
Nationalism in the Twentieth Century by Anthony D. Smith, 1979.
International Political Science Review Volume 1 by the International Political Science Association, 1980.
Human Inquiry by Peter Reason and John Rowan, 1981.
Revolutions and Revolutionists by Robert Blackey, 1982.
Budaya Politik dan Pembangunan Ekonomi by Albert Widjaja, 1982.
The British Political Tradition by W. H. Greenleaf, 1983.
Old and New Questions in Physics, Cosmology, Philosophy, and Theoretical Biology edited by Alwyn van der Merwe, 1983.
Science and Public Policy, Volumes 11-12 by The Science Policy Foundation, 1984.
Gleichheit oder Freiheit? by Erik von Kuehnelt-Leddihn, 1985.
Annals of Theoretical Psychology, Volume 5 edited by Leendert P. Mos,1986.
The Suppressed Madness of Sane Men by Marion Milner, 1987.
Second Chance in Education edited by Dan Inbar, 1990.
Contemporary Political Ideologies: a Comparative Analysis by Lyman Tower Sargent, 1993.
An Introduction to Problems in the Philosophy of Social Sciences by Keith Webb, 1995.
Ideologie und Utopie by Karl Mannheim, 1995.
Political Research Quarterly, Vol. 50, No. 4, December 1997.
Ideologies and Political Theory: A Conceptual Approach by Michael Freeden, 1998.
From Politics Past to Politics Future by Alan James Mayne, 1999.

Subpersonalities: the People Inside Us by John Rowan, 1990.
The Socialist Party of Great Britain by David A. Perrin, 2000.
Embodied Theories edited by Ernesto Spinelli and Sue Marshall, 2001.
The Selected Works of Arne Naess, Volume 1 by Arne Naess and Alan Drengson, 2005.
On Becoming a Psychotherapist by Windy Dryden and Laurence Spurling, 2006.
Ecology of Wisdom by Arne Naess, 2008.
Mirrors Tryptych Technology by Diana Silberman-Keller, 2009.
The Hands of the Living God: An Account of a Psycho-analytic Treatment by Marion Milner, 2010.
Community Practice: Theories and Skills for Social Workers by David A. Hardcastle, 2011.
Police Reform in China by Kam C. Wong, 2012.
Metaphor and Dialectic in Managing Diversity by Christina Schwabenland, 2012.

An Outline Sketch of Systematic Ideology

by George Walford

The Walsby Society

The Walsby Society is concerned with the theories of the late Harold Walsby. This pamphlet sketches Walsby's work in ideology; he also worked in other areas, notably in philosophy, mathematical logic, and the development of a dialectical algebra. His object, in all these studies, was to understand thought, thought itself and its effect upon the behaviour of people and of society.

The Walsby Society endeavours to carry on this work. It is a task which makes unusual demands upon those who would take part in it, for those who study thought must accept no restraints upon their own thinking. They must not regard any theory as proven, for this would be to exclude that theory from study. Those who would continue Walsby's work can accept even his own results only provisionally and tentatively. The greatest contribution anybody could make would be to prove all his results wrong; that would be a giant step forward along the path he strove to open up. The Walsby Society is concerned with Harold Walsby's work but is not committed to acceptance of it. All that is required of those who would work with the Society is that their activities should be relevant; opposition is as welcome as support.

This pamphlet is presented to the Walsby Society, but the Society has neither accepted nor rejected it. The Society, and the people connected with it, have complete freedom in regard to the propositions brought forward here, accepting or rejecting them as their own thinking shall indicate. The writer alone is responsible for every statement made.

So if this pamphlet should provoke you into opposing the theories it puts forward-well, that is one of the things it is meant to do. The Walsby Society will be glad to hear from you. Contact can probably be made through the source from which this pamphlet reached you. If not, then by writing to: The Bookshop, [address].

Introduction to An Outline Sketch of Systematic Ideology

The purpose of this essay is to present an outline sketch of the theory of ideology originated and developed by Harold Walsby. To present, not to establish. For support of what is set out here, for weight of evidence and answers to objections, the reader will need to look elsewhere, to its correspondence with his own experience, to Walsby's book, *The Domain of Ideologies*[1], or to the various works, papers and essays which undertake to establish different parts of the theory with argument and evidence? My intention here is only to present a general framework. I hope to make

---

[1] Published by William MacLellan, Glasgow, in collaboration with The Social Science Association, 1947.

it easier for the reader, particularly the newcomer to the subject, to appreciate the significance of the more specialised studies, to see where and how each of them fits in.

I should have liked to be able to claim that this essay, although limited in its aims, was accurate as far as it went. But this claim cannot be made. In reducing the complexity of ideological theory to this outline I have been unable to avoid distorting the outline itself. The reader will inevitably find, if he pursues his investigations, that as he encounters the material which has been excluded from this study it alters his view of what has been included. The most I can recommend is that the reader should treat this outline as a crutch, useful so long as he requires assistance but to be rejected when he has developed his own strength.

The theory of ideology to be presented is, with minor exceptions (and these, so far as it is possible to distinguish them, will be indicated), the work of Harold Walsby, who died in 1973. Walsby's starting-point was political. As a young man he was a revolutionary Socialist and, like others, became frustrated by the ineffectiveness of the revolutionary Socialist movement, by its failure to attract the support of the masses whose interests it claimed to represent. Unlike most frustrated Socialists Walsby did not sink into apathy. Finding the theory of the Left inadequate, both as an explanation of political behaviour and as a guide to action, he turned to a re-examination of political ideas, beliefs and theories. He did not approach them in the manner in which one political thinker usually examines the work of another, in the hope of finding weak points. Neither did he examine them as a philosopher examines theories, with the purpose of distinguishing the true from the false. He approached them in the objective fashion of one wishing to understand how these things come to be. He examined the ideas, beliefs and theories themselves, the relationships between them, and their influence upon human behaviour. The result was his theory of ideology. This was in the late 1930's and the early 1940's, when "ideology" was a less familiar term than it is today.

Harold Walsby's book, *The Domain of Ideologies*, was published in 1947. Before that the two main landmarks in the field were *The German Ideology*, by Karl Marx and Frederick Engels (written in 1845 / 6 but not then published), and *Ideology and Utopia*, by Karl Mannheim (first published, in German, in 1929). During the last two decades there has been a growing stream of books and papers on ideology which do not derive from Walsby's work or, directly, from that of Marx and Engels, but rather from Mannheim. He was the first to set eyes on one large section of the mountain range of problems presented by ideology, but he did not succeed in crossing it, and I have not found that the workers following in his path have got much farther. I have not read all their Works, but I have sampled them extensively ; they refer widely to each other and I have found no indication, in those I have read, that the others are significantly different. Many of these works are largely concerned with the question whether all, or only some, political theories, movements or organisations are influenced by ideology. Nearly all of them take it for granted that the influence of ideology is restricted to the political, or at most the societal field. None of them shows, as Walsby does, that ideology influences the whole of our intentional or purposive behaviour in every field of activity. For those who may wish to enquire further the best starting point is the most recent of these books: *Ideology and Politics*, by Professor Martin Seliger, 1976. It is with the intention of distinguishing it from these other approaches to the subject, none of which display, or seem to be capable of developing, the degree of comprehensiveness and integration found in Walsby's work, that the term "systematic ideology" has recently been adopted for the Walsbeian theory.

Ideology and the Left

Walsby came to develop a theory of ideology which relates to all our purposive or intentional behaviour, but his starting-point was political. The immediate cause of his rejection of Left-wing political theory was the crucial perception that the Left is not a specifically working-class movement nor the Right a specifically capitalist or bourgeois one. It is of course true that the numerical support enjoyed by the Left comes mainly from the working class, but so does that enjoyed by the Right. In this respect the two movements are alike. In countries which have universal adult suffrage, freedom of speech, of publication and political organisation, the Right consistently receives from the electorate, which is overwhelmingly of the working class, a number of votes which is at least comparable with, and is sometimes greater than, the number of votes received by the Left. The political division between Left and Right does not correspond with the economic division between workers and capitalists (or bourgeoisie) and, even after generations of Left-wing propaganda, is not coming to do so. The political struggles which occur in industrial or post-industrial states cannot be understood so long as they are assumed to be, or to reflect, or to express, struggles between economic classes. When political conflict becomes violent the battle is rarely, if ever, between capitalists and workers. It is Workers of the Left and workers of the Right who shoot one another.

The responsible spokesmen and thinkers of the Left are rarely so simpleminded as to claim that political allegiance is directly determined by class position; rather do they emphasise their rejection of "economic determinism." But they do assume *some* significant connection between the Left and the working class, although most of them are reluctant to specify exactly what it is (and those who do attempt to do so contradict each other). The Left is regarded as the working-class movement, having for opponent the Right, which is the movement of the capitalists, or the bourgeoisie, or the bosses. The Left account for political behaviour, however indirectly and with whatever refinements, by reference to the relationships between economic classes.

Walsby's work indicates that this view is not valid, that political conflicts cannot be understood in terms of the relationships between economic classes, that there is no significant correlation, direct or indirect, between the political structure of our society and its economic class structure. His explanation of the political structure which tends to appear, always displaying the same broad features, in every industrial or post-industrial country where universal adult suffrage and political freedom obtain, is that it is the expression, in the political field, of an ideological structure. The adherents of each political position extend over the whole range of economic positions. There are Right-wing workers and there are Left-wing capitalists. The adherents of each political position are not united by a common class position or a common economic interest. They are united by sharing a common ideology. We shall see that this means a good deal more than the self-evident proposition that the adherents of each political position have certain political ideas in common.

The Field of Ideology

The term "ideology," like the term "psychology," is used with three distinct meanings. It refers to that which is studied, to the activity of studying it, and to the theory resulting from that study. (Also, by analogy with "psychologist," we shall refer to the student of ideology as an ideologist).

Ideology (that which is studied) cannot be directly observed; its presence is inferred from observation of behaviour. It is, of course, by this means that we arrive at all our knowledge of the various structures internal to the living human being. We observe that what appears to be soft flesh maintains its form under stress, and from this we infer the presence of a rigid skeleton. We see that the emotional responses of each person are not random, and are not entirely determined by the stimuli applied, and from this we infer the presence of an emotional structure. We observe that the volitional behaviour, the considered statements and the purposeful actions, of each person are relatively predictable and consistent, and from this we infer the presence of a structure of ideas (a phrase which we will accept, for the moment, as referring to an ideology). In each instance, in order to render the observed behaviour comprehensible, we are obliged to infer the presence of an internal structure which significantly influences an area or class of behaviour. This willingness to recognise that action is significantly affected by internal factors, their presence implied by observable behaviour, is one of the things that distinguishes Walsby's approach from that of the behaviourists.

The behaviour which is influenced by ideology is volitional or intentional behaviour, the actions we perform upon consideration or with purpose. It is not necessary, for any action to be included in this field, that the consideration involved should be deep or prolonged, or the purpose a long-term one. If I move my lower leg as a reflex action after being struck below the knee that is not an item of volitional behaviour and is not influenced by my ideology. But if I perform exactly the same movement with the purpose of kicking a ball that is volitional behaviour and is influenced by my ideology. It is not necessary that the thought connected with the action should be valid. Men regulated their actions, over thousands of years, in accordance with theories which have since been proven false. Their actions rank, none the less, as intentional and purposive, their behaviour comes within the field of ideology.

Assumption and Identification

The twin foundation stones of ideological theory are the associated concepts of *assumption* and *identification*.

Assumption: Ideology is one of the studies concerned with thought, and it is general practice, among those who study thinking, to distinguish between the true and the false. It is, indeed, often taken for granted that the establishment of this distinction is the object and end of all such studies. The first hurdle which the ideologist has to surmount is that this distinction, if taken as an absolute one, is itself false. It is only relatively true. Nothing is absolutely true and nothing is absolutely false. All our knowledge, taking that term in its widest sense, to include not only facts but also theories, principles, opinions and so on, is relatively true, and all of it is relatively false. We do not know anything with unqualified, absolute certainty; there is no alleged fact which cannot be challenged, there is no proof which cannot be questioned. However strong the evidence there is always something pointing in the contrary direction, even if it be only the possibility of conceiving that things might be otherwise. The distinction between false and true, and also the distinction between what we know and what we "merely" assume, is a distinction only of degree. All our knowledge consists of assumptions, some of them more true than others, some of them better supported than others, but none absolutely true and none established with final and absolute certainty.

By accepting this the ideologist is relieved of the intolerable burden of deciding, for every proposition he encounters, whether it is true or false.

He knows in advance that it is an assumption, relatively true and relatively false, with some evidence in its favour and some against it. Knowing this, he can move on to examine its relationships with other assumptions and – his particular concern – its effects upon behaviour. When one is concerned to understand how assumptions influence behaviour then their truth or falsity is commonly irrelevant; men can be moved quite as powerfully by false assumptions as by true ones. Sometimes the degree of truth or falsity possessed by an assumption may be relevant, and then the ideologist is free to determine it, by the well-tried method of assembling and balancing the evidence on each side. But he is not bound to carry out this procedure-it is often a lengthy and difficult one-in every case before he can perform any other operations upon the assumption in question.

Ideology is concerned with our volitional behaviour, the actions we perform with purpose, and every action of this type implies the presence of assumptions. By acting in a certain way we show that we assume the situation in which we find ourselves to possess certain features.

As I sit here typing my behaviour implies that I assume the chair is strong enough to support me, the floor strong enough to support the chair, the joists the floor, and so on; a series of assumptions leading, eventually, to assumptions concerning the nature of matter and of the universe. All these assumptions are implied by my behaviour in sitting in the chair; if I did not make them I would not behave as I do, I would not sit in a chair if I did not assume it to be adequately supported.

At any time some assumptions are present to awareness and others are not, and rarely, if ever, can an action be fully explained by reference to assumptions of which the actor is aware. Assumptions not present to awareness are nearly always involved. Every time I speak to a person my behaviour implies the assumptions on my part that his hearing is good (which itself implies long chains of assumptions concerning his anatomy and physiology), that he understands the language I use (another long chain of assumptions concerning his education), that his attention is not concentrated elsewhere, that there is air between us to carry the vibrations produced by my vocal cords, that there is no louder noise to drown my voice, and so on – and on and on. This one common act implies assumptions almost without end[1]. All these assumptions are implied by my behaviour, but most of them are not present to my awareness. They cannot be; my capacity for awareness is limited, it cannot contain them all; it cannot even contain many of them without excluding that which I wish to speak about. Many, probably by far the greater part of the assumptions which are implied by, and which influence, our behaviour are necessarily not present to our awareness.

---

[1] *The Domain of Ideologies* pp. 103

Identification: We do not treat our assumptions as matters purely of logic, reason and evidence. We do not necessarily abandon an assumption because we have been compelled to admit that it runs against the balance of evidence, or is in contradiction either with itself or some other of our assumptions. We are not indifferent about our assumptions, we are attached to them.

A person is a whole comprising (among other features) a body and an ideology. Bodily experience affects the ideology – my experiences when I try to walk through a brick wall affect my assumptions concerning the nature of matter. Also, ideological structure affects physical behaviour – because my political assumptions have been changed I read different books and attend different meetings.

This interaction between body and ideology shows that, although distinct, they form parts of a whole, a whole we term a person, or a self. When our bodies are injured we say: "*I* was hurt," and similarly when our assumptions are attacked, we say: "He said *I* was wrong." Our behaviour implies that we regard our assumptions as parts of our selves, that we *identify* them with our selves, and our selves with them.

Identifications may be strong or weak. I have an assumption concerning the time of day, but my identification with it is weak; only a small amount of evidence – a glance at the clock – is required for me to abandon it and adopt another in its place. There are other assumptions to which I am strongly attached. It would take a great deal of evidence to induce me to abandon the assumption that I have, up till now at least, had two hands. In one case the attachment is weak, in the other it is strong, but both are, in ideological terminology, identifications.

"Assumption" and "identification" are used in systematic ideology as technical terms, and they are as neutral as any term in physical science. They state the presence of that to which they refer, and nothing more. With one exception, anything we may wish to convey about the strength, validity or other features of the assumption or identification in question must be explicitly added. The exception is that unless otherwise stated "identification" refers to a positive identification; if the one being referred to is negative it is necessary to say so. Some assumptions we favour, or support, or accept; others we disfavour, or oppose, or repudiate. In each case our behaviour is affected by the assumption; in each case we are attached to it, identified with it. But in one case the identification is positive, in the other it is negative.

There is one aspect of the behaviour connected with identification which can be misleading if one is not prepared for it. Completely positive identification with an assumption does not appear as enthusiastic support for it, and completely negative identification with an assumption does not appear as determined opposition to it. Support implies a distinction between supporter and supported, and hence something short of complete positive identification. Equally, opposition implies a connection between opposer and opposed, and hence something short of complete negative identification. Completely positive identification appears as unquestioning taking-for-granted, and completely negative identification appears as complete detachment from the assumption in question.

Most identifications are not completely positive or completely negative but only relatively one or the other. When the ideologist speaks of a positive or negative identification he means one which is relatively so; if the identification is completely negative or completely positive it is necessary to specify this.

When we support an assumption we imply that we are positively identified with it, and when we oppose one we imply that we are negatively identified with it. All identifications are either positive or negative, but many are not strongly one or the other, and for these the terms "support" and "opposition" may be too definite. There are a number of terms which can be used to describe the behaviour implying one or another degree of positivity or negativity, two of the most useful being "acceptance" and "concern." Acceptance of something implies positive identification with it, and a concern with something implies negative identification with it.

Thus the scientist is concerned with phenomena which are not understood, or not fully so, and this is a negative identification. His concern diminishes as understanding increases, and with the phenomena which are (or are believed to be) fully understood, so that he can accept them, his identification is positive.

When we say that concern indicates negative identification we are implying that a supporter of a movement, one whose identification with it is positive, is not concerned with it. This may contradict the usual view of the situation, but when we look more closely we see it is justified. The supporter does not wish to change the movement – if he did, he would not be an unqualified supporter. He accepts the movement as it is, is not concerned about it. What he wishes to change is the resistance the movement meets. He is opposed to this resistance, negatively identified with it, and it is with this resistance that he is concerned.

Definition of an Ideology

An ideology is usually thought of rather vaguely, as a person's system of ideas, or set of beliefs or values, or his general outlook, or mental attitude. We are now able to define it more sharply, as the set of assumptions with which he is identified.

Or, in Walsby's more extended definition:

> [An ideology is] the complete system of cognitive assumptions and affective identifications which manifest themselves in, or underlie, the thought, speech, aims, interests, ideals, ethical standards, actions – in short, the behaviour – of an individual human being! – *The Domain of Ideologies*, p. 97.

Ideological Groups

Each of us has his own unique ideology, his system of identifications and assumptions, which is not the same as that of anybody else. Also, some of the particular assumptions within each unique set are peculiar to the person concerned. Each of us has, for example, assumptions concerning his own body which he shares with nobody else. But each unique, personal set contains, in addition to particular assumptions, also more general assumptions, and these are held in common with other people. People identified with the same assumptions are thereby constituted an ideological group.

Some ideological groups are small, some are large. Their size depends primarily upon the generality of the assumptions which form the basis for the group, and the larger groups tend to be the more enduring. Thus the assumption "England" is more general than the assumption of any one address in England, and the group of people identified with England is both larger and more enduring than the group identified with any one English address.

It is common for assumptions to be included one within the other, as in this example, and sometimes this relationship extends through a series, producing a "Chinese-box" pattern of assumptions and also of the groups identified with them.

I assume I have pennies, you assume you have pound notes, and he assumes he has five-pound notes; no two of us have the same particular assumption. But we are all identified with the same general assumption: we all assume we have some English money. This common identification constitutes us an ideological group, and also distinguishes that group from another, composed of those identified with the assumption that they have some French money. These two groups, (together with other "national-money" groups) form a larger group whose members are identified with the more general assumption that they have some European money. As the assumptions become more general, so the groups become larger and fewer.

As one moves from more particular assumptions toward more general ones (and, accordingly, from smaller toward larger ideological groups), there comes a stage at which the assumptions and identifications under consideration are sufficiently general that each set, forming the basis of an ideological group, embraces, or is capable of being related to, the whole of existence, to the totality of both the social and the non-social worlds. At this level of generality the number of sets of assumptions, and consequently the number of ideological groups into which the population is divided, is small, and it is mainly these groups which are significant for the understanding of political behaviour. We shall refer to these universal systems of assumptions and identifications as "the major ideologies."

The Major Ideologies

Each of the major ideologies is capable of being expressed in relation to any field of existence, in relation to man, the natural World, the physical universe, the realm of ideas, and so on. In the field of abstract thought they appear as the different major philosophies (or classes of philosophies), and they can also be recognised as underlying the various religions, sciences, theories of art, etcetera. In relation to society they have been more fully developed than in some other fields, and here they appear as the familiar major political positions.

The main components of each of these systems of highly general assumptions have been distinguished, and it is accordingly possible to study, so to speak, the major ideologies "themselves," independently of their expressions in relation to particular fields of activity. They are seven in number and are entitled, respectively: protostatic, epistatic, parastatic, protodynamic, epidynamic, paradynamic, metadynamic[1]. As these names indicate, one of the main features by which each of them is distinguished is its assumption concerning the predominance of one or another form of the static or the dynamic principle in the world, and we shall discuss them firstly from this angle, taking the opportunity at the same time to indicate the political viewpoint especially associated with each ideology.

Protostatic: Those identified with this ideology imply by their behaviour their identification with the assumption that reality is static (or would be so if it were not interfered with). The only changes acceptable are those seen as tending to produce a static condition. The declaration by the Nazis of their intention to establish a

---

[1] These terms were not used by Walsby: they are a recent introduction.

state which should endure unchanged for a thousand years was calculated to obtain support from the protostatics[1].

Epistatic: Those identified with this ideology imply by their behaviour their identification with the assumption that although reality is predominantly static (or would be so if it were not interfered with) yet the static situation is often most effectively preserved by compromise with the dynamic principle. This ideology appears in the political field as Conservatism[2], with its willingness to accept changes which are in accordance with tradition or the wish of the people generally, or which will tend to avert greater changes. The attitude of Conservatism toward change can perhaps be described as reluctant flexibility.

Parastatic: Those identified with this ideology imply by their behaviour their identification with the assumption that change is a necessary part of existence but within a static framework. Changes are freely accepted, even promoted, provided they are improvements or adjustments, not affecting the basis of the structure concerned or the essence of the situation. This ideology appears in politics as Liberalism, which is concerned with progress, with perfecting the present social system, but is not concerned to transform this system into a different one.

With the three ideologies above, and the groups identified with them, we have a situation we have met before. Each of them has its own particular assumption concerning the form or degree of staticism which predominates in the world, but all of them are identified with the general assumption that it is the static and not the dynamic principle which predominates. Accordingly these three ideological groups together form a larger group; this group, and the ideology with which it is identified, Walsby terms *eidostatic*.

The next three major ideological groups are each identified with their own assumptions concerning the form or degree of the dynamic principle which predominates in the world; each of them is identified with the general assumption that it is the dynamic and not the static principle which is predominant, and accordingly these three ideological groups together also form one larger one; this group, and the ideology with which it is identified, Walsby terms *eidodynamic*[3].

Protodynamic: Those identified with this ideology imply by their behaviour their assumption that change is (or ought to be) universal and that it is (or ought to be) gradual, evolutionary rather than revolutionary. This ideology appears in politics as Labour-Socialism.

Epidynamic: Those identified with this ideology imply by their behaviour their identification with the assumption that change is (or ought to be) universal and fundamental, the appearance that anything may give of being static being a superficial illusion. Change, furthermore, is (or should be) not merely gradual

---

[1] The protostatic ideology is very much more important than appears from this brief notice; *The Domain of Ideologies* Part I is largely devoted to it.

[2] Throughout this paper names of political parties or movements are to be read as: "The party (or movement) which is known in Britain as. . . " The ideological equivalents are to be found in all industrial or post-industrial states where they are not suppressed, but they commonly bear different names and often exhibit other differences also. It is partly in order to avoid losing our main theme in these complications that this paper is written largely in terms of Left and Right.

[3] *The Domain of Ideologies* Part II Chapter 7.

and continuous but includes also discontinuities, revolutions, and it is changes of this type which are most highly valued. This ideology appears in politics as Communism.

Paradynamic: Those identified with this ideology imply by their behaviour their identification with the assumption that change is (or ought to be) universal and abolitionary. The state should not be maintained, adjusted, reformed or revolutionised, but abolished. This ideology appears in politics as Anarchism.

Each of the six groups mentioned above tends to assume that its own ideology is wholly and exclusively true. Like other assumptions this is more often implied than directly expressed. In politics the members of each group endeavour to establish a form of society which shall embody only their own assumptions. In other areas the members of each group assume or endeavour to demonstrate the exclusive validity of views or theories expressing their own assumptions, and to show that those expressing other assumptions are unscientific, or false, or wicked, according to the categories used in the particular field of activity.

Evidently, it is not possible that every one of these major ideologies should be wholly and exclusively true. If one is true then the others are false, or if all are relatively true then all are relatively false. But each ideology, and each assumption of each ideology, influences the behaviour of the group identified with it, confirming something mentioned earlier: the power of an assumption to influence behaviour does not depend upon its truth.

There is still one more major ideology to be brought forward:

Metadynamic: Those identified with this ideology imply by their behaviour that they are not exclusively identified with any one of the various forms of either the static or the dynamic principle but with all of them.

A short diversion is necessary, to avoid appearing wilfully mysterious. Although we do not go into the question in this essay, each of the major ideologies is particularly fitted, by correspondence between its basic assumptions and the basic structure of a certain field of existence, to perform a certain part of the total range of activities needed for the effective functioning of the social organisation[1]. The sphere of existence with which the metadynamic group is, by the nature of its basic assumptions, particularly associated, is the ideological field itself. This group, being concerned with the study of ideologies, is not identified with this or that assumption concerning a particular form of the static or the dynamic principle but with all the assumptions concerning either of them exhibited by the other major ideologies. In the field of politics this ideology does not appear as a separate movement or organisation but as a concern with the relationships between the other major ideologies, their political expressions, and the groups identified with them. The presence of the metadynamic ideology also answers the question whether there can be further ideologies extending the range beyond those given here; the answer is, briefly, that at this point the series returns upon itself. There is little point in going into further details here since the whole of this essay is an exposition of the metadynamic ideology.

---

[1]This was clearly implied in Walsby's work but, apart from some brief references, was not made explicit. [...] I emphasise here that the functional division between ideologies does not correspond to the division between economic classes.

Ideological Development

The order in which the major ideologies have been presented, running from protostatic to metadynamic, is not an arbitrary one. This is the order in which they
succeed each other in the development of the individual. We all begin life as
protostatics, some remain in this phase and others become epistatics. Some remain
in this phase and others become parastatics, and so on through the series. With
each step some of the limitations of the previous phase are overcome and some
new limitations are incurred, and each step involves the attempt to repudiate the
assumptions of the previous phase[1]. Walsby traces the origins of this process in
the early experiences of the growing child[2] but we shall confine our attention to its
appearance in political and societal behaviour.

When we first emerge from family life into direct contact with the general social
system we have little or no historical perspective. We are aware that things are
happening around us, people moving and events occurring, but we have no reason
to assume that the general structure of society is changing. Neither, of course, do
we consciously assume it to be static; the question does not directly arise. But our
behaviour in this phase implies that we make the static assumption. When young
we do not readily think of our parents as having once been children, and still less
are we able to accept that the conditions of childhood in their youth may have
been different from those we have known. We all begin societal life with the static
assumption, we first encounter the world as protostatics.

Many of us retain this primary, more or less unqualified, identification with the
static principle throughout our lives, continuing to behave as though the general
structure of society never changed. Others find that as their experience grows they
are obliged to accept that significant changes in this structure do occur; changes,
for example, in laws and economic relationships. To this recognition there are two
possible responses; the list confirms the person in his protostatic identification, the
second takes him into the next phase of development.

The first of the two possible responses to the recognition of change is to maintain
identification with the static principle but now to engage in active defence of it.
Those who exhibit this response no longer merely take the static principle for
granted. Rather do they assert that the static principle is the right one, that the
dynamic principle is evil and to be resisted. This response, this active assertion
of the protostatic ideology, leads toward efforts to eliminate the assumed causes
of change – Jews, immigrants and agitators for example. Here we have the root
of the connection between the protostatic ideology and autocratic or totalitarian
movements; these all strive for elimination of iniiuences assumed to be making for
change. (I emphasise that not all protostatics behave in this way. It is also possible
for the protostatic not to recognise the existence of significant change, to maintain
his passive identification with the static assumption, and observation shows this to
be a common stance. The protostatic ideology is not to be equated with Nazism or
with Fascism).

The protostatic may recognise the existence of significant societal change or he
may not. If he does recognise it he may change from a passive mode to an active

---

[1] This attempt is never wholly successful; see "Personal Ideological Structure"
below.

[2] *The Domain of Ideologies* Part II Chapter 7.

one; he may start trying to prevent change and to eliminate the assumed causes of it. In either case he maintains his identification with the protostatic ideology. But there is another response open to him. He may recognise the existence of societal change and accept it, come to regard it as something real and necessary. In this case he ceases to be a protostatic and moves to the next phase of ideological development.

The person surrendering his identification with the protostatic assumptions does not, however, leap directly to full acceptance of the dynamic principle. He has taken only the first step on a long journey. The change in his ideology is a minimal one, extending only to the recognition that it is well to be somewhat flexible in the matter, that to maintain the static principle rigidly is often to ensure its defeat, and that it can best be defended by admitting, under careful control, some small element of dynamism. The protostatic becomes an epistatic, he comes to identify with the major ideology which appears in the political field as Conservatism, accepting such changes as are in accordance with tradition, or will serve to avoid greater changes, and displaying towards the static-dynamic issue, as in other connections, a willingness to compromise.

The epistatic phase is not the end of the process. Some do remain in this phase but others move on to the parastatic ideology. The process can be followed (although with some complications) through the whole ideological series to the metadynamic phase, but enough has been said to enable us to bring out the point with which we are immediately concerned. This is that the presence, in the ideology of a person, of a modified form of the static assumption, implies that he was previously identified with an unmodified form of it. The nature of the epistatic ideology implies that those identified with it were previously identified with the protostatic. When the major ideologies are arranged in the order: protostatic, epistatic, parastatic, protodynamic, epidynamic, paradynamic, metadynamic, then the presence of a person at any point in the series shows him to have passed through the preceding phases.

One point which arises here is that we see ideology to be more than a complicated way of putting things that could equally well be expressed in political terms. It is, obviously, not the case that every Anarchist has been a Communist, every Communist a Labour Socialist, and so on. What ideological theory tells us is that every person identified with any ideology in the series from protostatic to metadynamic has been previously identified with the preceding ones in the series. He may or may not have expressed any of these identifications in the political field.

Intellect
As one moves along the range from protostatic toward metadynamic so the original identification with the static principle comes to be replaced by identification with dynamism.

There are other ideological features which follow a similar course of development as one moves along the ideological range, and in the next section we shall briefly discuss some of these, not following out their full development from one major ideology to the next but indicating the general course followed by each feature through the ideological series. These features are the identification with intellect, the group and cosmic situations, and individualism and collectivism, political and economic. I begin with intellect.

The identification with intellect and intellectuality is negative at the protostatic end of the range and becomes positive as one approaches the metadynamic. Nazism repudiates intellect and intellectuality, Anarchism accepts them[1]. It is necessary to distinguish between "intellect" and "intelligence[2]." The relationship between the two is complex and difficult, and they are commonly confused. All I can do here is to stress that ideological theory does not suggest that those toward the protostatic end of the range are any less intelligent, less sharp or quick of mind (or less capable of acquiring knowledge) than those toward the metadynamic end. What it asserts is that the former tend to accept non-rational factors as guides to action while the latter are concerned that their behaviour should be logically consistent and capable of being justified by reason.

Nazism (protostatic) claims to be guided by non-intellectual factors such as blood, race, the Will of the Leader. Toward the other extreme Anarchists (paradynamic) take it for granted that their behaviour should be governed by intellectual considerations; they devote much time and effort to study, argument and discussion, to ensuring that their behaviour shall be intellectually justifiable. The intervening ideologies display greater or lesser concern with intellect according to their situation in the range, the epistatic or Conservative, for example, being more intellectual than the protostatic or Fascist but less so than the epidynamic or Communist, who in turn is less so than the paradynamic or Anarchist.

The Group Situation

The environment in which we live can be divided in many ways. For the ideologist one significant division is between the social group and the rest of the environment. The two main ideological classes, eidostatic and eidodynamic, each display a characteristic pair of identifications, one with the social group (Walsby terms this the *group situation*), and the converse identification with the environment external to the social group (Walsby terms this the *cosmic situation*)[3].

The eidodynamics (Socialists, Communists, Anarchists) regard the existing social structure as the main source of the ills from which we suffer. They do not ascribe war, poverty, insecurity and the rest to the will of God, or the natural aggressiveness of man, or to natural law, or to any other extra-social factor, but to "the contradictions of' capitalism" or some other feature of our social organisation. They maintain that in order to improve human conditions we must reform, revolutionise or abolish existing society. They experience existing society as a hostile presence. They are opposed to it. They exhibit *negative identification* with it. As, in the Anarchist phase, this identification approaches complete negativity it tends to turn from concern into repudiation; Anarchists are not interested in the possibilities of reforming, or even of revolutionising, existing society. They would abolish it.

The eidostatics appearing in the political field as the Right exhibit the converse attitude toward the existing social structure. They are *positively* identified with it. We mentioned earlier that positive identification, when complete, does not appear as enthusiastic support. Active support implies recognition of a distinction

---

[1] *The Domain of Ideologies* Part I Chapters 3, 4.

[2] *The Domain of Ideologies* pages 22 - 24.

[3] *The Domain of Ideologies* pp. 134 et seq.

between supporter and supported, and hence something short of a completely positive identification. Those most completely identified with their social group (in this connection usually the nation), are not the outspoken patriots but those who take their membership of the group, and their compliance with the implied conditions of membership, completely for granted, and it is those at the eidostatic end of the range, the protostatics, who tend to behave in this way.

Among the more moderate eidostatics, the Conservatives and Liberals, the identification is less exclusively positive; there is some tendency toward recognising the group as something distinct from the person and, consequently, for the decision to support it to become a conscious choice. But even in this phase the social structure is not seen as the decisive factor in the human condition. Rich and poor alike, the Right tend to regard poverty as a result of extra-social factors – natural law, luck, personal qualities or the will of God – and consequently as something which just has to be accepted. They do not see poverty as the Left do, as a result of specific social conditions which can be altered. As Dr. Johnson expressed it: "How small, of all that human hearts endure / The part that laws or kings can cause or cure." This assumption is clearly distinct from the one with which the Left are identified, that laws, if not kings, can cause or cure a great deal.

In connection with the existing social structure, as elsewhere, negative identification tends to produce active concern, moving toward repudiation, and eventually detachment, as the identification becomes completely negative, and positive identification tends to appear as acceptance, becoming unquestioning as the identification approaches complete positivity.

The Cosmic Situation

When we turn to consider the respective identifications of the two main ideological classes with the non-social world (what Walsby terms their cosmic situations), we find a reversal of the identifications which they respectively exhibit with existing society. The eidostatics, (positively identified with existing society), are *negatively* identified with the non-social world, and the eidodynamics, (negatively identified with existing society), are *positively* identified with the non-social world.

The Left regard existing society as the source of poverty, insecurity, war, and the other major ills from which we suffer. They regard the non-social world in much the same way as the Right regard the social, as something presenting no particular problems and exercising no very great effect, either for good or ill. They are, for example, greatly concerned with poverty. In combating it they concentrate their efforts upon ensuring a more equitable distribution of the commodities available (an intra-social matter) rather than upon producing a greater supply of commodities (an activity directed toward the non-social world, the source of raw materials). Their behaviour implies that they assume the non-social world to be so far under control that it presents no serious problems. As they sometimes phrase it: "the problem of production has been solved." The Left, the eidodynamics, display toward the non-social world that attitude of acceptance, of taking for granted, that we have come to recognise as indicative of positive identification.

The eidostatics, on the contrary, tend to see the non-social world as the source of the ills from which we suffer, and accordingly it is toward this world that their efforts are mainly directed. They tend to concern themselves with efforts to establish and exercise control of the non-social world, sometimes by prayer, sometimes by industry.

They concern themselves with the production of goods, an activity directed toward the non-social world, rather than with questions concerning the fairness of their distribution within society. Toward the non-social world the Right display that active concern which we recognise as indicative of a negative identification.

Political Individualism and Collectivism

The ideologist does not dispute the general opinion that the ideas of the Right are different from those of the Left, but he does add something to it. Right and Left, eidostatics and eidodynamics, not only have different ideas, they also have different ways of thinking. As Walsby phrases it, they differ not only in the *content* but also in the *form* of their thought. The thinking of the Right tends toward agreement, toward acceptance of the prevailing opinion and toward compliance with authority. It tends toward fusion. The thinking of the Left tends in the opposite direction, toward disagreement, independence of thought, and resistance to authority. It tends toward fission.

These tendencies Walsby names, respectively, political (as distinct from economic) collectivism and political individualism. As is commonly the case with the features which distinguish the various ideologies, each of them is to be observed in the purest form toward the appropriate end of the range, political collectivism among protostatics and autocratic movements, political individualism among extreme eidodynamics.

The intermediate ideologies exhibit a greater or lesser tendency toward political collectivism or political individualism according to their position in the range. Nazism was explicitly and emphatically opposed to political individualism. The establishment of a totalitarian state required the elimination of independent thinking. The Nazis burnt books, imposed political control on the teaching given in the universities, killed, suppressed or expelled those holding political beliefs other than their own, and suppressed or banished those displaying mental independence even in what might appear to be neutral fields, such as art and literature.

In ideological terms they endeavoured to suppress all ideologies other than the protostatic. Nazism exhibited, in a virulent form, the absence of restraint, the identification with unmodified assumptions, characteristic of the protostatic phase. As one moves away from this end of the range through the more moderately eidostatic phases, epistatic and parastatic, the identification with political collectivism, and the opposition to political individualism, becomes less intense. Freedom of the press and of research come to be accepted, tolerance and the rule of law replace the demand that the individual should submit without reservation to the state. But even in these phases there is no doubt which way the balance of identification lies. Among Conservatives and among Liberals the assumption is that tradition, loyalty and submission to authority should take precedence over independent thinking as guides to action, and these are all forms of political collectivism.

This contrasts with the behaviour exhibited at the eidodynamic end of the range. As we move from Labour-Socialism, through Communism to Anarchism, so the tendency towards, and the influence of, collective thinking diminishes and independent thinking comes increasingly to be accepted as a valid guide to social action, until with Anarchism it becomes explicit that the individual is to be subjected to no authority or influence whatever, but is to decide his own course of action for himself.

One apparent anomaly needs mentioning. It is in the Communist movement, rather than among the eidostatics, that supporters are required to accept a prescribed "party line" under pain of disciplinary action, and this may seem to run against our connection of the eidodynamic ideologies with independent thinking. We need only comment that the eidostatic organisations do not need to impose such a requirement; their members rarely display a tendency toward independent thought strong enough to need restraining.

The term "individual" usually means an individual person, but this is not the only sense in which it may be used. We may equally well speak of individual families, individual parties, movements, firms, teams, crowds and so on. We may speak not only of biological but also of social individuals. Every distinct group is a social individual, and in political affairs (and also in economic affairs) it is these, rather than the biological individuals, which are the relevant units, the biological individual being a special case, a group consisting of one member. The proposition, therefore, that political individualism is exhibited by the eidodynamics, is not invalidated by the observation that Communists, or Anarchists, although perhaps displaying greater personal independence of thought than do Liberals, or Conservatives, yet accept the same general assumptions as other Communists or Anarchists, and to this extent may be said to think collectively. It is not only the Communists and Anarchists as separate persons who display political individuality, but also the Communist and Anarchist movements. Where the eidostatic movements tend to be supportive of the general society and, in time of stress, to submerge in it such individuality as they may at other times exhibit, the eidodynamic movements, Socialism, Communism and Anarchism set themselves up against the general society and the more extreme of them, at least, continue this opposition even in time of stress, as when the continued existence of the community is threatened by an enemy. They behave toward it (and also toward each other) as separate individuals.

See also *The Domain of Ideologies* Part I Chapter 6 and 7.

Economic Individualism and Collectivism

In the economic field the situation of the ideologies, as regards collectivism and individualism, is the reverse of that in the political field. The eidostatics exhibit *economic individualism* and the eidodynamics exhibit *economic collectivism*.

It is commonly accepted that the transition, which is occurring in Britain and other western democracies (and which has already occurred in the Communist countries), from private ownership of the mills, mines, factories and other major components of the productive system, to their ownership by the state and control by bodies representing the state, is a change from capitalism to (or toward) socialism. This may or may not be so; it depends on the meaning given to "socialism." What is definite is that this transition is not a change from economic individualism to economic collectivism. In the economic field as in the political field, the individuals in question are groups; there they were parties or movements, here they are firms, corporations, boards, industries. The change from ownership and control by independent persons (so far as that system ever existed; most economic organisations of any size always have been owned and controlled by groups) to state ownership and control by groups appointed by the state, is a change from one form of economic individualism to another. The various boards, corporations and so on which operate "state capitalism" and similar systems are just as much separate individuals –

mutually exclusive, often competitive and sometimes hostile individuals – as the individual capitalists or individual boards of directors ever were. They act as independent individuals toward each other, toward the community as a whole, and toward each member of the community.

Economic collectivism is (or rather, if it were ever to be established on any large scale it would be) something different from this. It is a system whereby the means of production as a whole are owned and controlled by society as a whole, each person having free access to the means of production (and hence to their products) by virtue of his membership of the owning and controlling community.

Personal Ideological Structure

Any reader who accepts – even if only provisionally – the theories brought forward in the preceding pages, and sets out to test them against his own observations, will quickly encounter gross discrepancies. The protostatics present no great problem; it will be found that their behaviour does, if not in all details then at least when taken as a whole, or over a period, exhibit predominantly the features these theories would lead us to expect. The first indication of trouble is the observation that the adherents of all other ideologies display, for much of the time and over large areas of activity, behaviour which is indistinguishable from that of the protostatics.

We all spend much time in eating, travelling, casual conversation, watching films or television, engaging in sports or attending entertainments (Frederick Engels was a keen fox-hunter), and these are all activities which imply identification with protostatic assumptions, with low intellectuality and political collectivism. Even in the act of verbally expressing our eidodynamic assumptions we have no choice but to demonstrate our protostatic identification with the general social group; we are obliged to use the common speech.

As one enquires further the discrepancies between theory and observation become more extensive. Each of the major ideological groups behaves in a way implying identification not only with its own ideology but also with all ideologies lying to the protostatic side of its own position. The discrepancy between ideological theory (as so far presented), and observable behaviour, becomes more severe as attention moves toward the eidodynamic end of the range until, with the paradynamics, we ind that the behaviour predicted by theory is, for some of them, a rare occurrence in their lives. Quite often we would need to spend long periods, sometimes years, observing the behaviour, including the speech, of a paradynamic before encountering any item of behaviour implying identification with the assumptions we have listed as distinctive of this ideology.

The difficulty is resolved when we take into account a feature which ideological development shares with some other developmental systems. This is that the development is from less to more complex, one aspect of the increasing complexity being the retention, within each successive phase as it emerges, of the main features of the less complex phases in the system. Thus the broadest of all developmental systems moves from the physical through the organic to the human; in this system man is the most complex phase, and he is so partly because he is not merely, or purely, human but incorporates also the main features of the organic and physical phases. He is a man and an animal and a physical object. In the ideological series each phase beyond the protostatic is not merely, or purely, epistatic, or parastatic, and so on, but is epistatic and protostatic, parastatic and epistatic and protostatic, until, at the eidodynamic extreme, the metadynamic is also paradynamic and epidynamic and protodynamic and parastatic and epistatic and protostatic. Each of us is identified with every ideology on the protostatic side of the most eidodynamic one implied by our behaviour, although it is this most eidodynamic one which determines our ideological classification.

Social Ideological Structure

The ideological structure of society is, in this respect, parallel with that of each person. In order to maintain expression of any ideology a society, like a person, must maintain expression of all those ideologies which lie to the protostatic side of it in the range. To show this for each ideology is a long, complicated and difficult task, and one which has not yet been carried out in full detail. [...] Here we shall speak only in general terms, showing briefly the grounds for accepting that the general eidostatic phase is not, as it is sometimes thought to be, an obsolescent survival but has to be accepted as a functional constituent of any society which is to maintain the eidodynamic phase; we shall indicate the grounds for believing the conception of a purely eidodynamic society to be an illusion.

The eidostatic ideologies are negatively identified with the non-social world and the eidodynamic ideologies are negatively identified with the social world. Active concern with any object or class of objects, the impulse to work on it and establish or increase control over it, goes with negative identification with it. We find, accordingly, that the eidostatic ideological groups tend to direct their energies toward the non-social World; it is this world they regard as the source of the ills, the problems and difficulties from which we suffer, and it is this world they regard as needing attention.

The eidodynamics, on the contrary, display negative identification with the social world; it is this world they regard as the source of the ills, the problems and difficulties from which we suffer and it is therefore toward this world that their energies are directed.

A society which has its attention directed entirely outward toward the non-social world, an exclusively eidostatic society, may survive. A society which has its attention directed entirely toward its own structure, a purely eidodynamic society, cannot do so.

Every society, if it is to survive, must ensure that its people are fed. This requires the direction of energy and attention toward the natural, the non-social world, it requires eidostatic behaviour. If the people are to do more than barely survive then many other material commodities must also be provided, and all of them require, for their production, eidostatic behaviour. We can conceive of a society in which these activities would not be necessary, but as a practical matter, if we are concerned with the well being of our children and our grandchildren and their immediate descendants, then we have to accept that most of the energy of our society, now and in the foreseeable future, will need to be directed toward the non-social world. This is to say that it will need to be expended in behaviour implying identification with the eidostatic ideologies.

These ideologies have to be accepted as functioning constituents of our society in the economic field. If our society is not to be a repressive one (and the eidodynamic assumptions exclude political repression) then those identified with these ideologies, now recognised as socially necessary, must be accorded means of expression for their assumptions in politics and in societal activities generally. We have to accept the continuing existence, in the political field and elsewhere, of eidostatic opinion in something like its present strength.

Conclusion to An Outline Sketch of Systematic Ideology

Let us assume the reader has found this outline sketch acceptable, that he has moved on to some of the studies which undertake to establish various parts of the theory and has found those also acceptable. Let us assume that he accepts, provisionally at least, the theory of systematic ideology. What effect will this have upon him personally? How will it influence his political views, his attitudes and expectations? It will produce a change more revolutionary than any he has previously experienced. He will not "change sides" as he may have done in the past. Instead, he will reject the conception of politics as a field in which one chooses a side, accepts this or that view and repudiates the others.

He will recognise that the field of ideology, and of social and political belief and action connected with ideology, is not a field which is dominated by arbitrary subjective choice. Neither is it a mere reflection or superstructure, governed by the events occurring in some other field; ideology is not merely an epiphenomenon of economic processes. Ideology is, like economics, psychology, biology and other such fields, a relatively independent area. It exhibits phenomena peculiar to itself, entities and events which are systematically related one to another, and processes which follow recognisable laws. All of these require, for their full comprehension, study of the internal relationships of the field itself, as well as study of the influence exercised by adjoining fields.

The study of ideology is still in a very early phase; the systematic ideologist is still able, for the most part, to speak only in general terms, and there are wide areas of activity which have not yet undergone even a preliminary ideological survey. But one conclusion which has been solidly established, receiving further confirmation from each study of particular areas, is the presence in our society of an ideological structure, exercising an influence which is not yet generally recognised.

I have tried to outline this structure, presenting, very briefly, each of the major ideologies, mentioning some of the more significant relationships between them and indicating that there is reason to regard each of them as a necessary functional constituent of modern industrial or post-industrial society. In the broadest terms, a society which is to endure must be supplied and maintained, and with these functions the eidostatics are concerned. If the society is to endure in the face of accelerating technological development then it must not only be supplied and maintained, it must also be constantly reformed and, on occasion, revolutionised, and with this the eidodynamics are concerned. If a modern society is to endure it needs eidostatics and eidodynamics, and when one enquires more closely then it is found that not only these two great ideological classes but also each one of the major ideologies is a necessary functional constituent of a modern society.

This is not generally recognised. Among all the different major political parties, movements, positions and theories there is not one which presents the others as being equally necessary with itself. Present systems of government vary, but they all have one thing in common. They all operate on the exclusive principle, they all assume that one ideology must prevail to the exclusion, more or less complete, of all others.

This assumption produces the greater part of the conflict, national and international, which not only deprives us of the benefits which modern society, with its productive systems, is capable of providing, but even puts our continued existence at risk. It does so because it ignores the ideological structure. The major ideologies, and the groups identified with them, being functionally necessary constituents of our society, cannot be eliminated. They can, for a time and to an extent, be suppressed, (at least in their overt political expression), but the effort involved produces stresses which become more unacceptable as our society becomes more integrated and the power of weapons increases.

The theory of systematic ideology indicates that we have to accept the range of major ideologies, and the groups identified with them, as enduring features of our society. This points to the conclusion that an adequate political structure would be one in accordance with the ideological structure, one which recognised that the major ideologies, and the major ideological groups, are complementary, rather than merely opposed, one to another. It is a conclusion which amounts to nothing more – and nothing less – than the recognition that if we are to survive we shall need to adapt our political system to the ideological realities.

In closing, let us recall what underlies the polysyllabic abstractions we have been using. "Ideological groups," "negative identifications," "economic individualism;" these, and similar terms, are only shorthand descriptions of ways in which people behave. It is people who form ideological groups, and it is people who form society and its ideological structure. When we speak of establishing a political system consonant with the ideological structure this is only to say that an adequate political system would be one that works with, and not against, the way in which people in our society behave.

Afterword

by Trevor Blake

THE *Domain of Ideologies* by Harold Walsby was first published in a single, small impression in 1947. It measures 7.5 inches vertically and 5 inches horizontally and includes 231 numbered pages. It is bound in blue cloth and was issued with a dust jacket. Between August 1992 and June 1994, a photocopy edition of the first impression was offered by George Walford. Although the book is regularly cited by scholars, it has never been reprinted – until now. This new impression is the first since 1947. This new impression includes several features not found in the first, including a previously unpublished photograph of the author, a new index, a new bibliography, and a selection of works that cite *The Domain of Ideologies* by Harold Walsby.

Harold Walsby was born in 1911. He earned his living most of his life as an artist. He was a member of the Socialist Party of Great Britain (SPGB) in the late 1930s. It was during his time in the SPGB, approximately 1938, that he met George Walford. The two sought to resolve some of the paradox of socialism, such as how socialism claimed to be of great benefit to the majority but was consistently rejected by the majority. Their conclusions led them to part with the SPGB. Between 1941 and 1943 they and others published under the names Democratic Union and The Absolutists. In 1943 they settled on the Social Science Association (SSA) as the name for their group, and they published under this name as late as 1963. The Social Science Association published pamphlets, magazines, and *The Domain of Ideologies*. In a letter to Trevor Blake dated 13 February 1993, George Walford wrote: "The *D of I* was written in 1947, and this has to be allowed for when reading it; the amount of attention paid to Nazism now seems less justified than it did two years after the war, Freud no longer possesses the stature he did then, and other things have changed – you will probably be more alive to them than I am."

Some time between 1950 - 1951 Walsby was employed as an instructor at Braziers Park in Ipsden. His friendship with Walford and others endured, but increasingly he devoted his writing to other interests. The Walsby Society was founded in 1953 by George Walford and others to encourage Walsby to continue his earlier interests. The Walsby Society sometimes met at Braziers Park, but it is not clear that Walsby attended his own Society. The group never succeeded in drawing Walsby himself back to his earlier interests. Walsby returned to the Socialist Party of Great Britain under a pseudonymn. The Walsby Society held lectures, and published pamphlets and magazines. Walsby taught at Braziers Park until his death in 1973.

A series of memorial lectures were given in Harold Walsby's name between 1974 and 1978. Between 1973 and 1979, disagreements about systematic ideology arose within the Walsby Society. Some appear to have remained closer to Walsby's ideas, while George Walford appears to have used Walsby's ideas as a basis for further inquiry. In brief, Walsby claimed that all individuals begin as Eidostatic and some become Eidodynamic; Walford claimed "in the behaviour of individual people psychological influences often predominate over ideological ones[1]." In 1977 Walford wrote, and the Walsby Society published, the pamphlet *An Outline Sketch of Systematic Ideology*. *An Outline Sketch* is included here as a summary of systematic ideology to that point, and as the dividing line between Walsby's theory and Walford's take on Walsby's theory. In October 1979 Walford began to publish his magazine *Ideological Commentary* (*IC*). He continued publishing *IC* until his death in 1994. The theory of Harold Walsby found in *The Domain of Ideologies* was investigated from 1947 to the late 1970s. From the late 1970s onward, the theory of George Walford (always quick to credit his friend and mentor) has defined systematic ideology.

The Domain of Ideologies is the foundation document of systematic ideology[2]. Walsby's theory of ideology is an entirely different take than Marx' claim that ideologies are always and only false (unless they are Marxist ideologies). Walsby's theory pre-dates similar schools of thought, such as postmodernism and the Situationist International. *The Domain of Ideologies* is also an early work by an enthused young man, one who apologizes for the structure of his own book in his own Foreword. For a more contemporary understanding of systematic ideology, read *Beyond Politics* by George Walford.

---

[1]"Meet Systematic Ideology." *Ideological Commentary* Number 64, June 1994.

[2]Walsby had no particular name for his theory. The earliest reference to Walsby's theory as systematic ideology occurs on a postcard dated 26 April 1961.

Index